FOUNDATIONS of CULTURAL COMPETENCY

Dr. Tanis King Starck

Published by Montezuma Publishing.

Please direct comments regarding this product to:

> Montezuma Publishing
> Aztec Shops Ltd.
> San Diego State University
> San Diego, California 92182-1701
> 619-594-7552

or email: *montezuma@aztecmail.com*

website: www.montezumapublishing.com

Production Credits
    Production mastering by: Ryan LaMar
    Quality control by: Steve Murawka

Publishing Manager: Kim Mazyck

ISBN-10:   0-7442-7209-2
ISBN-13:   978-0-7442-7209-3

Copyright © 2017 by Montezuma Publishing and the author(s), Dr. Tanis Starck . The compilation, formatting, printing and binding of this work is the exclusive copyright of Montezuma Publishing and the author(s), Dr. Tanis Starck . All rights reserved. No part of this work may be reproduced, stored in a retrieval system, or transmitted in any form or by any means, including digital, except as may be expressly permitted by the applicable copyright statutes or with written permission of the Publisher or Author(s).

All copyrighted materials contained herein are reprinted with the express written permission of the original copyright holder. Acknowledgments and copyrights used by permission appear at the back of the book, which constitutes an extension of the copyright page. It is a violation of the law to reproduce these selections by any means whatsoever without the express written permission of the copyright holder(s).

Every effort has been made to trace all the copyright holders. But if any have been inadvertently overlooked, the publisher will be pleased to make the necessary arrangements at the first opportunity.

TABLE OF CONTENTS

1. Introduction 1
2. Chapter 1: Defining Cultural Competency 19
3. Chapter 2: Developing Cultural Awareness 31
4. Chapter 3: Learning About Your Culture 41
5. Chapter 4: Cultural Competency Models 67
6. Chapter 5: Understanding Your Worldview 79
7. Chapter 6: Racial Identity Models 91
8. Chapter 7: Racism 109
9. Chapter 8: Oppression 119
10. Chapter 9: Power and Privilege 133
11. Chapter 10: Culturally Distinct Groups - Native Americans 165
12. Chapter 11: Culturally Distinct Groups – African Americans 189
13. Chapter 12: Culturally Distinct Groups – European Americans (White) 209
14. Chapter 13: Culturally Distinct Groups – Middle Eastern 215
15. Chapter 14: Culturally Distinct Groups – Asian Americans 227
16. Chapter 15: Culturally Distinct Groups – Latino Americans 241
17. Chapter 16: Culturally Distinct Groups – LGBTQ+ 255
18. Chapter 17: Conclusion 267

INTRODUCTION

INTRODUCTION

By the end of this module, participants will be able to:

Define cultural competence.

Discuss the stages of cultural competence.

Differentiate between cultural competence, cultural awareness and cultural sensitivity.

Define stereotype, prejudice, ethnic identity and worldview.

Explore several tools for cultural self-assessment.

Assess and evaluate own level of personal competence.

Participants will understand:

Courageous conversations about race and the impact of race on institutional structures are a first and necessary step in eliminating gaps in achievement

Conversations about race should lead each of us to examine our work. We will discover what we do not know and what we need to know to assure that Black and Latino students succeed academically, socially and emotionally. As we use this new knowledge and practice, the quality of education for all students will increase.

Our perceptions of others are expressed through communication, behaviors, and practices of relationship building. Each of these behaviors directly impacts student and adult ability to take risks, work hard, be resilient, and achieve.

Essential Questions:

What skills, knowledge, behaviors and attitudes do I need to be a culturally competent leader?

_____
_____
_____

2. How does race matter in our current political/social climate?

3. Is a high achieving institution high achieving if segments of the population consistently under-perform?

4. What behaviors support or undermine the academic, social, and emotional growth of students of color?

5. What are the indicators that show we are experiencing success in eliminating racial gaps in academic achievement?

_____
_____
_____
_____
_____
_____
_____

Participants will know that:

1. Conversations about the impact of race on learning and achievement may not be comfortable but they are necessary to eliminate race as a predictor of academic success

2. Culture and the lenses through which we see others impact our behaviors and our perceptions.

3. Each of us must confront our own attitudes, values, and biases that influence student success.

4. Perception of race continues to be a factor in the achievement of students.

5. In order to provide a responsive education, we within the learning community must uncover and identify our personal attitudes related to the race, culture, and language experiences students bring to the classroom.

Participants will be able to:

- Practice courageous conversations about the impact of race on academic success
- Think about and plan how to use the knowledge gained for greater student success
- Identify culturally responsive behaviors that contribute to the success of all students and the elimination of the achievement gap

- Sustain conversations that will impact policies, practices, and procedures that eliminate race as a predictor of success

Prior Knowledge and Skills Needed to Achieve Desired Outcomes:

Ability to work in teams
Empathy/Caring
Commitment—heart, spirit, and energy
Desire for equity for all students
Openness to change
Willingness to follow steps for courageous and difficult conversations

- To stay engaged
- To speak your truth
- To experience discomfort
- To accept and expect non-closure

GUIDELINES for DIALOG

1. Speak from your own experience. Use "I" language.

2. Be present, listen, and respect others when they are talking.

3. Practice timely attendance.

4. Participate to your fullest ability--community growth depends on the inclusion of every individual voice.

5. Always feel free to pass, to not speak or participate.

6. Do not be afraid to respectfully challenge

CULTURAL COMPETENCE: AWARENESS (Adapted from Sue & Sue)

1. The culturally competent professional is one who has moved from being culturally unaware to being aware and sensitive to his or her own cultural heritage and to valuing and respecting differences.

> ▶ The professional has begun the process of exploring his/her values, standards and assumptions about human behavior.
>
> ▶ Rather than being ethnocentric and believing in the superiority of his or her group's cultural heritage (arts, crafts, traditions, language), there is acceptance and respect for cultural differences.
>
> ▶ Other cultures and sociodemographic groups are seen as equally valuable and legitimate.

2. The culturally competent professional is aware of his or her own values and biases and how they may affect minorities.

> ▶ The professional actively and constantly attempts to avoid prejudices, unwarranted labeling, and stereotyping. (e.g., African Americans and Latino Americans are intellectually inferior and will not do well in school, that Asian Americans make good technical workers but poor managers, that women belong in the home or that the elderly are no longer useful in society).
>
> ▶ Culturally competent professionals try not to hold preconceived limitations and notions about culturally diverse people.
>
> ▶ The professional actively challenges their assumptions; tries to find effective ways to work cross-culturally; and monitors their functioning via consultations, supervision, and professional development.

3. Culturally competent professionals are comfortable with differences that exist between themselves and others in terms of race, gender, sexual orientation, and other sociodemographic variables. Differences are not seen as negative.

> ▶ The culturally competent professional does not profess color blindness or negate the existence of differences in behavior, attitudes, cultural norms, beliefs, etc., among different groups.

4. The culturally competent professional is sensitive to circumstances (personal biases; stage of racial, gender, and sexual orientation identity; sociopolitical influences, etc) that may dictate referral of a student to a member of his or her own socio-demographic group or to another professional in general.

> ▶ A culturally competent professional is aware of his or her limitations and is not threatened by the prospect of seeking assistance and support from others. However…

▶ This principle should not be used as a cop-out for the professional who does not want to work with culturally diverse students, staff and families, or who do not want to work through their own personal hang-ups.

5. The culturally competent professional acknowledges and is aware of his or her own racist, sexist, heterosexist, or other detrimental attitudes, beliefs, behaviors, and feelings.

▶ A culturally competent professional does not deny the fact that he or she has directly or indirectly benefited from individual, institutional, and cultural biases and that he or she has been socialized into such a society. As a result, the culturally competent professional inherits elements in the socialization process that may be detrimental to culturally and ethnically diverse students, staff and families.

▶ Culturally competent professionals accept responsibility for their own racism, sexism, heterosexism, etc., and attempts to deal with them in a non-defensive, guilt-free manner. They have begun the process of defining a new non-oppressive and non-exploitive attitude. In terms of racism, for example, addressing one's Whiteness (e.g., white privilege) is crucial for effective teaching.

CULTURAL COMPETENCE: KNOWLEDGE (Adapted from Sue & Sue)

1. The culturally competent professional must possess specific knowledge and information about the particular group he or she is working with.

▶ The professional must be aware of the history, experiences, cultural values, and lifestyles of various socio-demographic groups in our society.

▶ The professional understands the idea that the greater the depth of knowledge of one cultural group and the more knowledge the professional has of many groups, the more likely it is that he/she can be effective in his/her role.

▶ Thus, the culturally competent professional is one who continues to explore and learn about issues related to various minority groups throughout his or her professional career.

2. The culturally competent professional will have a good understanding of the sociopolitical system's operating in the United States with respect to treatment of marginalized groups in our society.

▶ The culturally competent professional understands the impact and operation of oppression (racism, sexism, heterosexism, etc.), the politics of the education system, and the racist, sexist, and homophobic concepts that have permeated institutions.

▶ Especially valuable for the educator is an understanding of the role that ethnocentric mono culturalism plays in the development of identity and worldviews among minority groups.

3. The culturally competent professional must have clear and explicit knowledge and understanding of the generic characteristics in individuals from diverse ethnic, racial and socioeconomic backgrounds.

> ▶ These encompass language factors, culture-bound values, and class-bound values. The professional should understand the value assumptions (normality and abnormality) inherit in education and how they may interact with values of the culturally different student, staff, and families.

> ▶ In some cases, applying theories or models to a particular group, may limit the potential of persons from different cultures. Likewise, being able to determine those that may be useful to culturally and ethnically diverse individuals is important.

4. The culturally competent professional is aware of institutional barriers that prevent some diverse students and families from accessing services.

> ▶ Important factors include the location of services, the formality or informality of décor, advertising services and events in English only, where event are publicized, the availability of minorities, school climate, hours and days of operation, transportation, childcare, and how services/events are viewed by some cultures.

CULTURAL COMPETENCE: SKILLS (Adapted from Sue & Sue)

1. At the skills level, the culturally competent professional must be able to generate a wide variety of verbal and nonverbal responses.

> ▶ Mounting evidence indicates that different groups may not only define problems differently from their majority counterparts, but also respond differently to teaching styles.

> ▶ Thus, the wider the repertoire of responses and pedagogy the educator possesses, the better educator he or she is likely to be.

> ▶ We can no longer rely on a very narrow and limited number of skills in teaching. We need to practice and be comfortable with a multitude of teaching styles and modalities.

2. The culturally competent professional must be able to send and receive both verbal and nonverbal messages accurately and appropriately.

> ▶ The culturally skilled professional must be able not only to communicate (send) his or her thoughts and feelings to the student/family, but also to read (receive) messages from the student/family (verbal and nonverbal messages).

> ▶ Sending and receiving a message accurately means the ability to consider cultural cues operating within a setting.

▶ Accuracy of communication must be tempered by its appropriateness. In many cultures, subtlety and indirectness are appreciated. Likewise, others appreciate directness and confrontation.

3. The culturally competent professional is able to exercise a variety relationship building skills with his or her students, family members and co-workers when appropriate.

▶ This implies that teaching may involve out-of-classroom strategies including; attending special events, outreach, acting as a change agent, and home/community visits.

4. The culturally competent professional is aware of his or her helping style, recognizes the limitations that he or she possesses, and can anticipate the impact on culturally diverse students.

▶ When teaching-style adjustments appear too difficult, the next best thing to do may be to

a) acknowledge your limitations and consult with other professional
b) anticipate the impact your limitations have on others; c) participate in Culturally Relevant Professional Development.

▶ These things may communicate several things to your culturally diverse students, families and coworkers: first that you are open and honest about your style of communication and the limitations or barriers they may potentially cause; second, that you understand enough about their worldview to anticipate how this may adversely affect them; third, that as a professional, it is important for you to communicate your desire to help despite your limitations; and fourth, that you care enough to do something about it.

Confidentiality Agreement

Pre-Test

CULTURAL SCAVENGER HUNT

Chat with the people in the room. Find people who have had the following experience. Have them sign their name in the appropriate blank. You may only use each name once!

_____ knows a folk dance.

_____ has been to an American Indian pow-wow.

_____has cooked or eaten ethnic food this last month.

_____ can say "hello" in 4 different languages.

_____ has sat under a palm tree.

_____ has attended a service of a religion other than theirs

_____ knows what Kwanzaa is.

_____ has relatives who came through Ellis Island.

_____ knows when Ramadan was this year.

_____ has had to utilize crutches, a wheel chair, or cane

_____ has been to a bar mitzvah or bat mitzvah.

_____has been to more than 5 countries.

_____ has studied a foreign language.

_____ can name 4 different kinds of bread from other cultures.

_____ knows where their ancestors came from.

_____ knows American Sign Language or someone who speaks it.

_____ has attended a Quinceañera.

_____ was born in a different state.

_____ knows what a yarmulke is.

_____ knows when African American History Month is.

_____ knows who Cesar Chavez is.

_____ has been to Mesa Verde.

_____ celebrated the Chinese New Year.

_____ has walked in the MLK march once in their life.

Cultural Scavenger Hunt Activity Reflection

Academic Diversity Activities: Exploring Diversity

Part 1

Answer the following questions about yourself.

1. What is your ethnic background? _____

2. Where were your parents and grandparents born? _____

3. How much education do your parents have? _____

4. What languages do you speak? _____

5. What is your biggest challenge this semester? _____

6. What is one of your hopes or dreams for the future? _____
   _____

7. What do you enjoy most? _____
   _____

8. What is your most important value and why? _____
   _____

9. What is one thing you are proud of? _____

10. What is one thing people would not know about you just by looking at you? _____
    _____

11. Have you ever experienced discrimination because of your differences? If so, briefly describe this discrimination. _____
    _____

Part 2

Meet with two other students you do not know. Introduce yourself and share answers to the above questions. Your instructor will ask you to share your answers to the following questions with the class

1. List three interesting things you learned about other persons in your group.

   _____

   _____

   _____

2. Did you change any assumptions you had about persons in your group?

   _____

   _____

   _____

Exploring Diversity Activity Reflection

References

Drozd, D. (2015, November 24). UNO Study: Fertility Rate Gap Between Races, Ethnicities is Shrinking. Retrieved July 26, 2017, from https://www.unomaha.edu/news/2015/01/fertility.php

Delpit, L. (2006). *Other Peoples Children: Cultural Conflict in the Classroom.* The New Press.

Sue, D. W., & Sue, D. (1999). *Counseling the culturally different: theory and practice.* New York: J. Wiley & Sons.

Lynch, E. W., & Hanson, M. J. (2011). *Developing cross-cultural competence: a guide for working with children and their families.* Baltimore, MD: Paul H. Brookes Pub.

A More Perfect Union: Building an Education System that Embraces All Children. the Report of the Nasbe Study Group on the Changing Face of Americas School Children. (2001). National Association of State Boards of Education.

CHAPTER 1
DEFINING CULTURAL COMPETENCY

DEFINING CULTURAL COMPETENCE and RELATED TERMINOLOGY

What is Cultural Competence?

A set of congruent behaviors, attitudes, and policies that come together in a system, agency, or among professionals and enables that system, agency, or those professionals to work effectively in cross–cultural situations. It is a complex integration of cultural knowledge, cultural awareness or sensitivity, attitudes, cultural skills, and cultural encounters (Cross, Bazron, Dennis, & Isaacs, 1989; Isaacs & Benjamin, 1991).

The level of knowledge-based skills required to provide effective disaster assistance to survivors from a particular ethnic or racial group (U.S. Department of Health and Human Services, Health Resources and Services Administration [DHHS, HRSA], 2001). (Starck, T. 2011 And Her Name Was Katrina: Life After the Storm)

The ability of systems to provide care to clients with diverse values, beliefs and behaviors, including tailoring delivery to meet clients' social, cultural, and linguistic needs (Betancourt, Green & Carrillo, 2002).

"Understanding the importance of social and cultural influences on (disaster survivors') beliefs and behaviors, considering how these factors interact at multiple levels of the (emergency response) system, and devising interventions that take these issues into account to assure quality delivery (of disaster response and recovery interventions) to diverse populations" (Betancourt, Green, Carrillo & Ananeh-Firempong, p. 297, 2003). (Starck, T. 2011, And Her Name Was Katrina: Life After the Storm)

General Characteristics of Cultural Competence?
(Source: DHHS, HRSA)

1. Understanding, appreciating, and respecting the cultural differences and similarities within, among and between diverse groups.
    2. Respecting individuals and cultural differences.
    3. Implementing a trust-promoting method of inquiry.
4. It is not limited to race and ethnicity. It includes acculturation level, social class, sexual orientation, age, religion and gender.

What does it mean to be Culturally Competent?

Culturally competent individuals have the capacity to function effectively in other cultural contexts and within the context of culturally integrated patterns of human behavior as defined by a group.

Common terms associated to Cultural Competence?

To increase cultural competence and create an awareness of sociopolitical forces that result in multicultural and diversity barriers, it is important to understand the following terms:

Culture - The thoughts, communications, actions, customs, beliefs, values, and institutions of racial, ethnic, religious, or social groups. It refers to integrated patterns of human behavior that include the language, thoughts, communications, beliefs, values, and institutions of racial, ethnic, religious, or social groups (DHHS, CLAS, 2001).

Competence - Having the capacity to function effectively as an individual and an organization within the context of the cultural beliefs, behaviors and needs presented by consumers and their communities (DHHS, CLAS, 2001).

Stereotype - Fixed ways of thinking about people that do not allow for individual variation.

Prejudice - A negative attitude directed toward people, simply because they are members of a specific social group.

Discrimination - A negative action toward members of a specific social group.

Racism - Attitudes toward members of a racial group that incorporate both egalitarian social values and negative emotions, causing one to avoid interaction with members of the group.

Sexism - Any attitude, action or institutional structure that subordinates a person because of her or his sex.

Heterosexism - A system of cultural beliefs, values and customs that exalts heterosexuality and denies, denigrates and stigmatizes any non-heterosexual form of behavior or identity

DEFINITIONS

Ally – A member of the "majority" group who rejects the dominant ideology and takes action against oppression or of a belief that eliminating oppression will benefit the target group and the minority group.

Anti-racism – Conscious and deliberate behavior that challenges the impact and perpetuation of racism and works to reverse the disparities that exist. Anti-racist practices in the school prepare students intellectually, socially, emotionally, and politically to live and work in a diverse and changing world.

Bias: An inclination of temperament or outlook; especially a personal and sometimes unreasoned judgment

Culture - Learned, dynamic behavior. The values, traditions, symbols, beliefs, and practices which are created and shared by a group of people bound together by such common factors as history, location, or social class. (Nieto)

Cultural Competence - The attainment of attitudes, skills, knowledge, and behaviors that enable staff and students to develop positive relationships and work effectively in cross cultural situations.

Discrimination– Unfair and often illegal, partiality, or bias in acts, policy, and/or patterns of behavior, that negatively impact the treatment of a person or group.

Equity- Providing each student with the individual support he/she needs to reach a common standard of performance. Equity is demonstrated explicitly by teachers through expectations, rigor, relevance to students' lives, and most of all, relationships with students.

Ethnicity

Ethnicity describes groups in which members share a cultural heritage from one generation to another (Robinson & Howard- Hamilton, 2000). Attributes associated with ethnicity include a group image and a sense of identity derived from contemporary cultural patterns (e.g., values, beliefs, and language) and a sense of history

Oppression – A form of domination and control that grants benefits and rewards to some people and denies the same access to others. Power – A socio-political process that refers to the capacity to effect changes and wields influence or thought.

Prejudice- Any preconceived opinion or feeling (favorable or unfavorable) formed without knowledge or thought. Privilege – A right or immunity granted as a peculiar or personal benefit, advantage, or favor. Privilege grants a set of benefits and system rewards to one group while simultaneously excluding other groups from accessing these advantages.

Race– Originally the term race was used to sort races on the basis of phenotypic or permanent physical characteristics; therefore, basis of physical differences. A socially constructed means of control that serves to perpetuate economic, social, political, psychological, religious, ideological, and legal systems of inequality.

Racial Identity Development – The process of defining for oneself the personal significance and social meaning of belonging to a particular racial group. (Tatum)

Racism– Beliefs and enactments of beliefs that one set of characteristics is superior to another set:

- The systematic mistreatment of certain groups on the basis of skin
- Color or other physical characteristics carried out by societal institutions or by people who have been conditioned by society, consciously or unconsciously, in harmful ways towards people of color.
- The combination of individual prejudice and individual discrimination, and institutionalized policies and practices that result in the unjustified negative treatment and subordination of members of a racial or ethnic group.

Social Construct – A concept or practice which may appear to be natural and obvious to those who accept it, but, in reality is an invention or artifact of a particular culture or society.

Stereotype – A set of beliefs, generalized about a whole group of people.

White Privilege - Special advantages or benefits of white persons. A right, advantage, or immunity granted to or enjoyed by white persons beyond the common advantage of all others; an exemption in many particular cases from certain burdens or liabilities. (Clark)

Worldview - Refers to attitudes, values, opinions, concepts, thought and decision making processes, as well as how one behaves and defines events.

PREJUDICE, DISCRIMINTION and RACISM
DO NOT REQUIRE INTENTION

Framework for Cultural Competency: Awareness Competencies

Conceptualizations of cultural competence have often used stage-wise developmental models and theories that assume that individuals start with a base level of functioning. With appropriate training and education, individuals, progress from these lower levels of understanding to increasingly more complex and differentiated modes of functioning. People operating at higher developmental levels generally possess more proficiency at a particular skill, such as developing cultural competence. The goal of cultural competence training programs is to develop in individuals and institutions levels of proficiency in:

- Understanding
- Accepting
- Working skillfully with culturally different students and their families

Elements of cultural competency

The culturally competent system would:

- Value diversity
- Have the capacity for cultural self-assessment
- Be conscious of the dynamics inherent when cultures interact;
- Have institutionalized cultural knowledge; and
- Have developed adaptations to diversity." (Terry Cross et.al. 1989)(2)
- Create natural, informal support networks within ethnic and culturally diverse communities.
- Build collaborations with neighborhood, civic, and advocacy associations, local and neighborhood merchants, ethnic, social and religious organizations, and spiritual leaders and healers.
- Regard community members as full partners in decision making.
- Knowledge, skills, and strategies should reciprocate among all collaborators and partners.
- Communities strive to enhance awareness of available services and resources in effort to strengthen access, quality, and effectiveness

Almost everything that we experience is shaped by the perceptions provided by our view of the world. Culture filters what we see and what we perceive. Culture determines the generally accepted definitions of social reality.

Stages of Cultural Competency Development

Stages of Cultural Competency
- Cultural Knowledge
- Cultural Awareness
- Cultural Sensitivity
- Cultural Competency

Cultural Knowledge:

Familiarization with selected cultural characteristics, history, values, belief systems, and behaviors of the members of another ethnic group (Adams, 1995).

Cultural Awareness:

Developing sensitivity and understanding of another ethnic group. This usually involves internal changes in terms of attitudes and values. Awareness and sensitivity also refer to the qualities of openness and flexibility that people develop in relation to others. Cultural awareness must be supplemented with cultural knowledge (Adams, 1995)

Cultural Sensitivity:

Knowing that cultural differences as well as similarities exist, without assigning values, i.e., better or worse, right or wrong, to those cultural differences (National Maternal and Child Health Center on Cultural Competency, 1997).

Cultural Competency:

Evolves over time through the process of attaining cultural knowledge, becoming aware of when cultural mores, values, beliefs and practices are being demonstrated, sensitivity to these behaviors is consciously occurring, and one purposely utilizes culturally based techniques in dealing with the workplace and with service.

Levels of Cultural Competency Development

Destructiveness:

Attitudes, policies and practices destructive to other cultures; purposeful destruction and dehumanization of other cultures; assumption of cultural superiority; eradication of other cultures; or exploitation by dominant groups. The complete erosion of one's culture by contact with another is rare in today's society.

Incapacity:

Unintentional cultural destructiveness; a biased system, with a paternal attitude toward other groups; ignorance, fear of other groups and cultures; or discriminatory practices, lowering expectations and devaluing of groups.

Blindness:

The philosophy of being unbiased; the belief that culture, class or color makes no difference, and that traditionally used approaches are universally applicable; a well-intentioned philosophy, but still an ethnocentric approach.

Pre-Competence:

The realization of weaknesses in working with other cultures; implementation of training, assessment of needs, and use of diversity criteria when hired; desire for inclusion, commitment to civil rights; includes the danger of a false sense of accomplishment and tokenism.

Competence:

Acceptance and respect for differences; continual assessment of sensitivity to other cultures; expansion of knowledge; and hiring a diverse and unbiased staff.

Proficiency:

Cultures are held in high esteem; constant development of new approaches; seeking to add to knowledge base; advocates for cultural competency with all systems and organizations.

References

Adams, D. L. (Ed.). (1995). Health issues for women of color: A cultural diversity perspective. Thousand Oaks, CA: Sage

Betancourt, J. R., Green, A. R., Carrillo, J. E., & Ananeh-Firempong, O. (2003). Defining cultural competence: a practical framework for addressing racial/ethnic disparities in health and health care. *Public Health Reports, 118*(4), 293–302.

Cross, T. L., Benjamin, M. P., & Isaacs, M. R. (1989). *Towards a culturally competent system of care*. Washington, D.C.: CASSP Technical Assistance Center, Georgetown University Child Development Center.

Journey towards cultural competency: lessons learned. (1997). Washington, D.C.?: Maternal and Child Health Bureau.

National Standards for Culturally and Linguistically Appropriate Services in Health Care: Final Report. (n.d.). *PsycEXTRA Dataset.* doi:10.1037/e568422010-001

NIETO, S. (1996). Affirming diversity: the sociopolitical context of multicultural education. New York: Longman.

New HRSA Activities to Link Individuals with Care and Prevention Services. (n.d.). *PsycEXTRA Dataset.* doi:10.1037/e359302004-003

Smedley, A. (1998). "Race" and the Construction of Human Identity. *American Anthropologist, 100*(3), 690-702. doi:10.1525/aa.1998.100.3.690

Tatum, B. D. (n.d.). Talking About Race, Learning About Racism: The Application of Racial Identity Development Theory in the Classroom. *Racism: Essential Readings,* 311-325. doi:10.4135/9781446220986.n31

CHAPTER 2
DEVELOPING CULTURAL AWARENESS

What is culture?

Culture can be defined as 'what we create beyond our biology. Not given to us, but made by us (Williams, in MacNaughton, 2010, p. 14). Using this definition, culture incorporates the scope of human diversity and ways of being, such as gender, ethnicity, class, religion, ability, age and sexuality. This means that as educators, we need to 'think about our own values, beliefs and attitudes related to diversity and difference and acknowledge and address any bias that we may hold'. As well as critically examining our own assumptions, 'cultural competence' requires us to take a strong approach to countering racism and bias when we encounter it. This is a long way from a 'live and let live' attitude. It involves making a conscious decision to promote children's cultural competence so that we can build a just and inclusive American society.

Being moral includes living the principles of justice. It involves making sure that everyone gets a fair go and that hidden attitudes to race, class and difference are de visible and challenged While cultural competence encompasses a wide spectrum of difference beyond race and ethnicity, those aspects are usually the first in our minds when we hear the term. As well, because we work with all cultures we have a special responsibility to contribute to America's reconciliation and equity agendas in relation to social change.

Culture is the total, generally organized way of life, including values, norms, institutions, and artifacts, that is passed on from generation to generation. Culture becomes our reality, the map that guides us. It's the window through which we view the world. To attack someone's culture, but not acknowledging its importance is to attack that person's innermost self. We ALL have a culture.

Cultural Awareness Self-Assessment Form

Please answer Yes or No to each of the questions.

1. I listen to people from other cultures when they tell me how my culture affects them._____

2. I realize that people from other cultures have fresh ideas and different points of view to bring to my life _____

3. I give people from other cultures advice on how to succeed in my culture and to the workplace. _____

4. I give people my support even when other members of my culture reject them. _____

5. I realize that people outside of my culture could be offended by my behavior. I've asked people if I have offended them by things I have done or said and have apologized whenever necessary. _____

6. I realize that when I am stressed out I am likely to make myself and my culture right and another culture wrong. _____

7. I respect my superiors (boss, teacher, supervisor, group leader, etc.) regardless of where he or she is from. I do not go over his or her head to talk to someone from my culture in order to try and get my way. _____

8. When I am in mixed company, I mix with everyone. I do not just stay with people from my culture, or only with people from the dominant culture. _____

9. I go out of my way to work with, recruit, select, train, and/or promote people from outside the dominant culture. _____

10. When people in my culture make jokes about or talk negatively about other cultural groups, I let them know that I don't like it._____

When culture is ignored, students are at risk of not getting the support they need, or worse yet, receiving assistance that is more harmful than helpful. It is a filter through which people process their experiences and events of their lives. It influences people's values, actions, and expectations of themselves. It impacts people's perceptions and expectations of others.

Culture gives context and meaning.

It is a filter through which people process their experiences and events of their lives. It influences people's values, actions, and expectations of themselves. It also impacts people's perceptions and expectations of others.

What is culture, and how do we humans acquire our cultures?

A good working definition is the following:

1. Culture is the learned and shared knowledge that specific groups use to generate their behavior and interpret their experience of the world.
2. It comprises beliefs about reality, how people should interact with each other, what they "know" about the world, and how they should respond to the social and material environments in which they find themselves.
3. It is reflected in their religions, morals, customs, technologies, and survival strategies.
4. It affects how they work, parent, love, marry, and understand health, mental health, wellness, illness, disability, and death.
5. Much of culture resides only in people's heads; thus, it is invisible and sometimes hard to detect.

One way to understand culture is to think of it as the "software" of the mind. Essentially, individuals are "programmed" by their cultural group to interpret and evaluate behaviors, ideas, relationships, and other people in specific ways that are unique to their group. Another excellent analogy for understanding the cultural process is to see culture as the "lens" through which people in a specific group view the world.

Culture is akin to being the person observed through a one-way mirror; everything we see is from our own perspective.

It is only when we join the observed on the other side that it is possible to see ourselves and others clearly – but getting to the other side of the glass presents many challenges.

(Lynch & Hanson 1992 Developing Cross Cultural Competence)

Slide Source: National Center for Cultural Competence, 2007

Culture exercises a kind of invisible control over members of a cultural group. Psychologists call this "internalizing" our cultural norms and concepts. We all do this very naturally. However, this process often has the effect of rendering our own culture invisible to us, though we can readily identify cultures that differ from ours.

Despite the invisibility of "software" or a "lens," a culture is clearly reflected outwardly in such things as how people behave, what they eat, how they dress, the tools they use, and the values and ideas they express. Nevertheless, it takes considerable introspection and self-analysis for individuals to discover how deeply and strongly their culture influences their own thoughts and behaviors. Because human beings in different parts of the world and in very different environments developed distinctively different cultures, they "see" and respond to the world in widely varying ways. Social scientists often call a group of people who share a culture an ethnic group. An ethnic group is a group socially distinguished or set apart by others or by itself, primarily on the basis of cultural or national-origin characteristics. Many often use the terms "ethnic group" and "cultural group" interchangeably. Most cultural groups tend to believe that how they see the world is correct, and how they believe and behave is what is most natural to human beings, that is, "human nature." However, in learning about culture, we need to understand that to have culture is human nature, but no specific culture is human nature! When people insist on their own culture as the only correct way to understand the world, they are said to be demonstrating ethnocentrism. It is easy to fall into this fallacious way of thinking. We all do it from time to time; however, the culturally aware person is far less likely to unthinkingly fall into this cognitive trap.

Definition/Framework	Author
"Culture is a set of meanings, behavioral norms, and values used by members of a particular society, as they construct their unique view of the world."	Alarcon, Foulks, & Vakkur (1998)
"Culture is conceived as a set of denotative (what is or beliefs), connotative (what should be, or attitudes, norms and values), and pragmatic (how things are done or procedural roles) knowledge, shared by a group of individuals who have a common history and who participate in a social structure."	Basabe, Paez, Valencia, González, Rimé, & Diener (2002)
"The term culture refers to social reality. It can be defined as a complex collection of components that a group of people share to help them adapt to their social and physical world."	Yamamoto, Silva, Ferrari, & Nukariya (1997)
"Culture is a shared pattern of belief, feeling, and knowledge that ultimately guide everyone's conduct and definition of reality."	Griffith & González (1994)
"Culture is a shared organization of ideas that includes the intellectual, moral and aesthetic standards prevalent in a community and the meanings of communicative actions."	LeVine (1984)
"Culture is a person's/group's beliefs, their interactions with the world, and how they are affected by the environment in which they exist."	Lotrecchiano (2005)
"Culture is an integrated pattern of human behavior which includes but is not limited to—thought, communication, languages, beliefs, values, practices, customs, courtesies, rituals, manners of interacting, roles, relationships, and expected behaviors of an ethnic group or social groups whose members are uniquely identifiable by that pattern of human behavior."	National Center for Cultural Competence (2001)
"Culture is a system of collectively held values, beliefs, and practices of a group which guides decisions and actions in patterned and recurrent ways. It encompasses the organization of thinking, feeling, believing, valuing and behaving collectively that differentiates one group from another. Values and beliefs often function on an unconscious level."	Sockalingam (2004)

References

Alarcón, D., Foulks, E. F., & Vakkur, M. (1998). *Personality disorders and culture: clinical and conceptual interactions*. New York: John Wiley & Sons.

Basabe, N., Paez, D., Valencia, J., Gonzalez, J. L., Rimé, B., & Diener, E. (2002). Cultural dimensions, socioeconomic development, climate, and emotional hedonic level. *Cognition & Emotion, 16*(1), 103-125.

Cross, T. L., Benjamin, M. P., & Isaacs, M. R. (1989). *Towards a culturally competent system of care*. Washington, D.C.: CASSP Technical Assistance Center, Georgetown University Child Development Center.

Delpit, L. (2006). *Other People's Children: Cultural Conflict in the Classroom*. The New Press.

Fox, R. W., & Lears, T. J. (1993). *The Power of culture: critical essays in American history*. Chicago: University of Chicago Press.

Griffith, E. E. H., & González, C. A. (1994). Essentials of cultural psychiatry. In C. Yudofsky, R. Hales, & J. Talbott (Eds.), *The American Psychiatric Press textbook of psychiatry* (2nd ed., pp. 1379–1404). Washington, DC: American Psychiatric Press.

LeVine, R. (1984). Properties of culture: An ethnographic view. In R. Schweder & R. LeVine (Eds.), *Culture theory: Essays on mind, self, and emotion*. Cambridge University Press.

Lotrecchiano, G. (2005, September 28). Definition of culture. Cited in a presentation, *Methods for cultural understanding: Assumptions and definitions of culture,* Washington, DC.

MacNaughton, G. (2010). *Shaping early childhood: learners, curriculum and contexts*. Maidenhead: Open University Press.

Moule, J., & Diller, J. V. (2012). *Cultural competence: a primer for educators*. Belmont, CA: Wadsworth.

National Center for Cultural Competence. (2001). Definitions of culture. Washington, DC: Author

Rokeach, M. (1960). *The Open and closed mind; investigations into the nature of belief systems and personality systems*. New York: Basic Books.

Sockalingam, S. (2004, September 10). Definition of culture. Cited in a presentation, *Diversity and culture,* Bethesda, MD.

Sue, D. W., & Sue, D. (1999). *Counseling the culturally different: theory and practice*. New York: J. Wiley & Sons.

Yamamoto, J., Silva, A., Ferrari, M., & Nukariya, K. (1997). Culture and psychopathology. In G. Johnson-Powell, & J. Yamamoto (Eds.), *Transcultural child development: Psychological assessment and treatment*. New York: Wiley

CHAPTER 3
LEARNING ABOUT YOUR CULTURE

Central to the concept of cultural competency is that it is a developmental process that evolves over an extended period. In order to respect and acknowledge differences, a person needs to know and accept himself or herself as a cultural being.

Self-assessment is not only for individuals, but it also expected of organizations in which individuals belong. Conducting cultural self-assessments by individuals and organizations is one of the key elements in achieving cultural competence

Both organizations and individuals are at various levels of awareness, knowledge and skill acquisition along the cultural competence continuum as self-assessment is an ongoing process, not a one-time occurrence. In this section, we will review some basic concepts of cultural competency, and introduce definitions of terminology commonly used in the discussion of cultural competence.

Self-awareness: Becoming aware of your own worldview

- Learning About Your Own Culture
- Understanding Your Personal Worldview
- Appreciating Your Own Multiple Identities
- Acknowledging Assumptions and Biases
- Accepting Responsibility and Tolerating Ambiguity
- Recognizing Limits of Your Competence

Exercise

LEARNING ABOUT YOUR OWN CULTURE

Think of yourself as a cultural being whose life has been influenced by various historical, social, political, economic, and geographical circumstances. This exercise will help you become aware of your historical, ethnic and cultural background.

1. Where were you born?

_____

2. Where did your parents grow up?

_____

3. Where did your grandparents grow up

_____

4. Where did you great-grandparents grow up?

_____
_____
_____
_____

5. What is your earliest memory as a family?

_____
_____
_____
_____
_____
_____
_____
_____
_____

6. What is your earliest memory of school?

_____
_____
_____
_____
_____
_____
_____
_____
_____

7. As a family, what events did you celebrate?

_____
_____
_____
_____
_____
_____
_____
_____
_____

8. Have you traveled or moved as a child? If yes, Where?

_____
_____
_____
_____
_____

9. Recall on international event that happened before you turned 18. Try to answer the following: Who was involved, what was the event, where did it happen, how did it happen, and why did it happen?

_____
_____
_____
_____
_____
_____
_____
_____
_____
_____

10. Recall an event that happened in the country where you were born, before you turned 18. Try to answer the following: Who was involved, what was the event, where did it happen, how did it happen, and why did it happen?

___

11. What is your earliest recollection as a member of a group?

___

12. What was your first job?

___

13. As an adult, what events or holidays do you currently celebrate?

___

Did You Know That...

1. Many immigrants may be reluctant to disclose personal information, fearing that by saying something wrong or revealing such information, they might create problems for their families? To ease such fear, educators should first explain why the information is needed.

2. Avoidance of eye contact may be a sign of respect? Culture affects how people use their eyes when they speak or listen.

3. Because Asian and Muslim children often experience cultural conflict when they are asked to hold hands with members of the opposite sex, they may refrain from participating in an activity?

4. Because teachers are often regarded as authority figures, students from many Asian and African countries and their parents are often reluctant to ask questions, share or challenge ideas, or talk about concerns they may have?

5. Family loyalty is an important part of the Latino culture and is given priority to the student's education.

6. In some cultures, dropping in without notice is the norm?

7. Misunderstandings due to cultural differences may act as obstacles to the delivery of optimal services to students and parents.

8. Most races are made up of many cultural and ethnic groups: Bantus and Zulus, for example, are cultural groups that belong to the Black race, and Hmong, Mien, and Zhuang are all cultural groups that belong to the Asian race. Clearly, these groups are culturally very different from each other because culture and ethnicity refer to the concepts inside people's heads, not to their physical characteristics. Moreover, a cultural group may be made up of persons from several races as with Puerto Ricans who can me of African, American Indian, White or mixed racial descent.

9. Because race is a socially defined construct used to categorize people by their physical characteristics, it is not surprising that different cultures have very different perspectives with respect to racial identifiers and to relations between people of different races.

10. Physical variations, most often in appearance, acquire distinct meanings and are linked to class or caste in various ways, depending upon the specific culture.

11. Someone classified as "Black" in the U.S., for instance, might be considered "White" in Brazil and "Colored" in South Africa. These meanings structure social relations, oftentimes resulting in stratification and discrimination over time.

12. Further, when a racial group is excluded or isolated from other groups within a culture, and the isolation continues over several generations, the group may develop a distinctive group identity that becomes a subculture within the larger culture. In this way, culture may become linked with race though the two are conceptually different.

13. A culturally aware individual will be knowledgeable about the interaction between culture and race, and be sensitive to the effect of his/her own culture on racial ideology, bias, and race relations.

CULTURAL COMPETENCY: DEVELOPING CULTURAL AWARENESS

Developing Cultural Awareness:

What is Cultural Awareness, Anyway? How do I build it?

Cultural Awareness is the foundation of communication and it involves the ability of standing back from ourselves and becoming aware of our cultural

1. **How do you see the world?**

2. **Why do you react in that particular way?**

Defining Cultural Awareness

According to Winkelman (2005), awareness of cultural differences and their impact on behavior is the beginning of intercultural effectiveness. He states that "cultural self-awareness includes recognition of one's own cultural influences upon values, beliefs, and judgments, as well as the influences derived from the professional's work culture"

- Cultural awareness can help us to:
  - Acknowledge how culture shapes their own perceptions;
  - Be more responsive to culturally diverse colleagues;
  - Be more sensitive and accessible as a mentor or supervisor;
  - Be alert to cultural differences and similarities that will present opportunities and challenges to working in a multicultural environment; and
  - Influence the next generation of professionals to be culturally aware as a prerequisite toward achieving cultural and linguistic competence.

- Cultural awareness includes:
  - Having a firm grasp of what culture is and what it is not;
  - Having insight into intracultural variation;
  - Understanding how people acquire their cultures and culture's important role in personal identities, life ways, and mental and physical health of individuals and communities;
  - Being conscious of one's own culturally shaped values, beliefs, perceptions, and biases;
  - Observing one's reactions to people whose cultures differ from one's own and reflecting upon those responses; and
  - Seeking and participating in meaningful interactions with people of differing cultural back- grounds.

Cultural awareness becomes central when we have to interact with people from other cultures. People see, interpret and evaluate things in a different ways. What is considered an appropriate behavior in one culture is frequently inappropriate in another one. Misinterpretations occur primarily when we lack awareness of our own behavioral rules and project them on others. In the absence of better knowledge we tend to assume, instead of finding out what a behavior means to the person involved.

Becoming aware of our cultural dynamics is a difficult task because culture is not conscious to us. Since we are born we have learned to see and do things at an unconscious level. Our experiences, our values and our cultural background lead us to see and do things in a certain way. Sometimes we have to step outside of our cultural boundaries in order to realize the impact that our culture has on our behavior. It is very helpful to gather feedback from foreign colleagues on our behavior to get more clarity on our cultural traits.

Projected similarities could lead to misinterpretation as well. When we assume that people are similar to us, we might incur the risk that they are not. If we project similarities where there are not, we might act inappropriately. It is safer to assume differences until similarity is proven.

Cultural awareness becomes central when we have to interact with people from other cultures. People see, interpret and evaluate things in a different ways. What is considered an appropriate behavior in one culture is frequently inappropriate in another one. Misunderstandings arise when I use my meanings to make sense of your reality.

Many Italians perceive US Americans as people who always work, talk about business over lunch and drink their coffee running in the street instead of enjoying it in a bar. What does it mean? Italians are lazy and American hyperactive? No, it means that the meaning that people give to certain activities, like having lunch or dinner could be different according to certain cultures. In Italy, where relationships are highly valued, lunch, dinner or the simple pauses for coffee have a social connotation: people get together to talk and relax, and to get to know each other better. In the USA, where time is money, lunches can be part of closing a deal where people discuss the outcomes and sign a contract over coffee.

Misinterpretations occur primarily when we lack awareness of our own behavioral rules and project them on others. In absence of better knowledge we tend to assume, instead of finding out what a behavior means to the person involved, e.g. a straight look into your face is regarded as disrespectful in Japan.

Becoming aware of our cultural dynamics is a difficult task because culture is not conscious to us. Since we are born we have learned to see and do things at an unconscious level. Our experiences, our values and our cultural background lead us to see and do things in a certain way. Sometimes we have to step outside of our cultural boundaries in order to realize the impact that our culture has on our behavior. It is very helpful to gather feedback from foreign colleagues on our behavior to get more clarity on our cultural traits.

Projected similarities could lead to misinterpretation as well. When we assume that people are similar to us, we might incur the risk that they are not. If we project similarities where there are not, we might act inappropriately. It is safer to assume differences until similarity is proven.

DEGREES of CULTURAL AWARENESS

According to Adler, there are several levels of cultural awareness that reflect how people grow to perceive cultural differences.

Stage 1:

My way is the only way - At the first level, people are aware of their way of doing things, and their way is the only way. At this stage, they ignore the impact of cultural differences. (Parochial stage)

Stage 2:

I know their way, but my way is better – At the second level, people are aware of other ways of doing things, but still consider their way as the best one. In this stage, cultural differences are perceived as source of problems and people tend to ignore them or reduce their significance. (Ethnocentric stage)

Stage 3:

My Way and Their Way - At this level people are aware of their own way of doing things and others' ways of doing things, and they chose the best way according to the situation. At this stage people realize that cultural differences can lead both to problems and benefits and are willing to use cultural diversity to create new solutions and alternatives. (Synergistic stage)

Stage 4:

Our Way - This fourth and final stage brings people from different cultural background together for the creation of a culture of shared meanings. People dialogue repeatedly with others, create new meanings, new rules to meet the needs of a particular situation. Increasing cultural awareness means to see both the positive and negative aspects of cultural differences.

In becoming culturally aware, people realize that:

- We are not all the same
- Similarities and differences are both important
- There are multiple ways to reach the same goal and to live life
- The best way depends on the cultural contingency.
- Each situation is different and may require a different solution.

How Culturally Aware Are You?

Please write to the following prompts:

- To what degree do you and your colleagues believe race impacts achievement?

_____
_____
_____
_____
_____
_____
_____
_____
_____

- To what degree has race been a factor in your academic/career pursuits?

_____
_____
_____
_____
_____
_____
_____
_____
_____
_____
_____
_____
_____
_____

- Can you think of a time in a personal or professional circumstance when race became a topic of conversation and you either actively changed the subject or avoided the conversation altogether? Please explain

_____
_____
_____
_____
_____
_____
_____
_____
_____
_____

- What do you believe caused you to react in this manner?

_____
_____
_____
_____
_____
_____
_____
_____
_____

HOW DO I MANAGE CULTURAL DIVERSITY?

We are generally aware that the first step in managing diversity is recognize it and learning not to fear it. Since everyone is the product of their own culture, we need to increase both self-awareness and cross-cultural awareness. There is no book of instructions to deal with cultural diversity, no recipe to follow. But certain attitudes help to bridge cultures.

- **Admit that you don't know**.

Knowing that we don't know everything, that a situation does not make sense, that our assumptions may be wrong is part of the process of becoming culturally aware. Assume differences, not similarities.

- **Suspend judgments.**

Collect as much information as possible so you can describe the situation accurately before evaluating it.

- **Empathy.**

In order to understand another person, we need to try standing in his/her shoes. Through empathy we learn of how other people would like to be treated by us.

- **Systematically check your assumptions.**

Ask your colleagues for feedback and constantly check your assumptions to make sure that you clearly understand the situation.

- **Become comfortable with ambiguity.**

The more complicated and uncertain life is, the more we tend to seek control. Assume that other people are as resourceful as we are and that their way will add to what we know. "If we always do, what we've always done, we will always get, what we always got."

- **Celebrate diversity.**

As professionals find ways of sharing the cultures of your diverse colleagues in your school/and or workplace..

Attitudes Toward Cultural Awareness

As your awareness of culture increases, your attitude toward cultural difference likewise evolves. The model summarized below, by Milton Bennett describes this journey from ethnocentrism to ethno relativism:

ETHNOCENTRISM

As your awareness of culture increases, your attitude toward cultural difference likewise evolves. The model summarized below, by Milton Bennett describes this journey from ethnocentrism to ethno relativism:

STAGE I: DENIAL

People in this stage don't really believe in cultural differences; they think people who are behaving differently don't know any better. These people tend to impose their own value system on others, knowing that they're "right "and these other people are "confused." They believe the way they behave is natural and normal and the way other people behave, if it's different, is wrong and misguided. These people are not threatened by cultural differences because they simply don't accept them. Generally, people in this stage have had limited contact with people different from themselves and thus have no experiential basis for believing in other cultures.

STAGE II: DEFENSE

These people have had an indication that their value system may not be absolute-and they're not happy about it. Unlike people in the denial stage, those in the defense stage believe in cultural difference and have accepted the reality of it, but they are deeply threatened by it and believe that other cultures are decidedly inferior. "This may be how things are, but it is not the way things should be." They know better than to try to impose their values on others, but they view other cultures negatively and prefer to have little or no contact with those who are different.

STAGE III: MINIMIZATION

People at this stage are still threatened by difference-that's why they try to minimize it-but they don't think that those who are different are inferior, misguided, or otherwise unfortunate. Rather, they believe that the differences are real but not especially deep or significant, that as different as people are, they are still more similar than dissimilar. We are different on the surface, but underneath we share many of the same values and beliefs. If people in the denial stage deny difference and people in the defense stage accept but demonize difference, then people in the minimization stage try to trivialize difference.

ETHNORELATIVISM

STAGE IV: ACCEPTANCE

These people accept differences as being deep and legitimate. They know other people are genuinely different from them and accept the inevitability of other value systems and behavioral norms. They still find some of these behaviors hard to deal with or accept, but they are not threatened by them nor do they judge them as wrong or bad. They do not normally adopt many of these behaviors for themselves nor necessarily adjust their own behaviors to be more culturally sensitive, but they have a more tolerant and sympathetic attitude. They are neutral, not positive, about differences. Difference is a fact of life.

STAGES V & VI: ADAPTATION AND INTEGRATION

In these stages, behaviors as well as attitudes, change. These people have gone from being neutral about difference to being positive. They not only accept cultural differences, but are willing and able to adjust their own behavior to conform to different norms. They are able to empathize with people from different cultures. In many ways, they become what are known as bi cultural or multi-cultural, effortlessly adjusting their behavior to suit the culture of the people they're with, "style switching," in other words. They do not give up their own or birth culture's values and beliefs, but they do integrate aspects of other cultures into it. In the integration stage, certain aspects of the other culture or cultures become a part of their identity.

EXERCISES ATTITUDES TOWARD CULTURAL DIFFERENCE

Part One

Think of these stages for each one and answer the questions in the spaces below

1. DENIAL

Can you think of anyone you know who is in this stage?

_____
_____
_____
_____
_____
_____
_____
_____
_____
_____

Have you ever exhibited any of the behaviors associated with this stage? If yes, briefly describe.

_____
_____
_____
_____
_____
_____
_____
_____
_____

2. **DEFENSE**

Have you ever exhibited any of the behaviors associated with this stage? If yes, briefly describe.

_____
_____
_____
_____
_____
_____
_____
_____
_____
_____

3. **MINIMIZATION**

Can you think of anyone you know who is in this stage?

_____
_____
_____
_____
_____

Have you ever exhibited any of the behaviors associated with this stage? If yes, briefly describe.

_____
_____
_____
_____
_____
_____

4. **ACCEPTANCE**

Can you think of anyone you know who is in this stage?

_____
_____
_____
_____
_____
_____

Have you ever exhibited any of the behaviors associated with this stage? If yes, briefly describe.

_____
_____
_____
_____
_____
_____
_____
_____
_____

5. ADAPTATION AND INTEGRATION

1. Can you think of anyone you know who is in this stage?

_____
_____
_____
_____
_____

2. Have you ever exhibited any of the behaviors associated with this stage? If yes, briefly describe.

_____
_____
_____
_____
_____

In general, what stage do you think you are in now? Why do you think so?

_____
_____
_____
_____
_____
_____

How did you move from the stage or stages you were in before to the stage you are in now?

_____
_____
_____
_____
_____

References

Adler, P. S. (1998). Beyond cultural identity: reflections on multiculturalism. Basic concepts of intercultural communication: Selected readings, 225–245.

Bennett, M. (1993). *Towards ethnorelativism: a developmental model of intercultural sensitivity*. S.l.: S.n.

Winkelman, M. (2005). *Cultural awareness, sensitivity and competence*. Peosta, IA: Eddie Bowers Pub.

CHAPTER 4
CULTURAL COMPETENCY MODELS

Bennett Model of Cultural Competence

1. There are many developmental models of cultural competence in the field. One commonly referenced model is the Bennett model, which was developed by Milton Bennett and consists of a continuum of six stages moving from "ethnocentrism" to "ethnorelativism."

2. This model, as is the case with most models, is valuable in that it provides a springboard for discussion.

3. Individuals and organizations may be at different points on the continuum depending on the diversity dimension in reference. For example, individuals may be at the Acceptance stage with reference to race, and at the Defense stage with reference to sexual orientation.

4. The ethnocentric stages are Denial, Defense, and Minimization. The ethnorelative stages are Acceptance, Adaptation, and Integration.

    1. In the first stage, Denial, an individual denies that cultural differences exist. This belief may reflect either physical or social isolation from people of different cultural backgrounds.

    2. In the second stage, Defense, an individual acknowledges the existence of certain cultural differences, but because those differences are threatening to his or her

own reality and sense of self, the individual constructs defenses against those differences. Bennett offers three commonly used defense mechanisms:

1. The first method of defense is denigration, or negative stereotyping, of another group.
2. The second defense, superiority, is where an individual places his or her group above another.
3. The third method, reversal, is less common. It involves the denigration of one's own culture and the idealizing of another.

3. The third stage in Bennett's model is Minimization. An individual in this stage acknowledges cultural differences, but trivializes them, believing that human similarities far outweigh any differences. The danger of this stage is that similarity is assumed rather than known. As Bennett writes, "In general, people who have experienced cultural oppression are wary of the 'liberal' assumption of common humanity. Too often, the assumption has meant 'be like me.'"

4. In the fourth stage, Acceptance, an individual recognizes and values cultural differences without evaluating those differences as positive or negative. This stage moves an individual from ethnocentrism to ethnorelativism. First comes a respect for cultural differences in behavior, and then a deeper respect for cultural differences in values.

5. In the fifth stage, Adaptation, individuals develop and improve skills for interacting and communicating with people of other cultures. The key skill at this stage is perspective-shifting, the ability to look at the world "through different eyes."

6. The final stage of Bennett's model is Integration. Individuals in this stage not only value a variety of cultures, but are constantly defining their own identity and evaluating behavior and values in contrast to and in concert with a multitude of cultures. Rising above the limitations of living in one cultural context, these individuals integrate aspects of their own original cultural perspectives with those of other cultures.

References

Bennett, M. J. (1993). Towards Ethnorelativism: A developmental model of intercultural sensitivity. In R. M. Paige (Ed.). Education for the intercultural experience. Yarmouth, ME: Intercultural Press.

Models of Cultural Competence

Conceptualizations of cultural competence have often used stage-wise developmental models and theories that assume that individuals start with a base level of functioning. With appropriate training and education, individuals progress from these lower levels of understanding to increasingly more complex and differentiated modes of functioning.

People operating at higher developmental levels generally possess more proficiency at a particular skill, such as developing cultural competence. The goal of cultural competence training programs is to develop in individuals and institutions levels of proficiency in:

> Understanding
>
> Accepting
>
> Working skillfully with culturally different students and their families

Although several cultural competency models exist, the foundations for this work are primarily based upon the work of Pedersen (1994), Mason, Benjamin, & Lewis (1996). And Sue and Sue (2003)

While Pedersen's model focuses more on changing awareness, knowledge, and skills relative to cultural competency Mason et al. focus more on creating culturally competent organizations and services through institutional and organizational responsiveness that emanate from changes in the individual .

All of these approaches are valid and important and, together, provide the theoretical and conceptual bases for this course.

Mason et al. (1996) outlined a cultural competence model in which individuals transition from damaging and mis-educative practices to professional practices that endorse culturally relevant service delivery models (Slide 11). This model consists of five stages or statuses, which include:

1. Cultural destructiveness
2. Cultural incapacity
3. Cultural blindness
4. Cultural pre-competence
5. Cultural competence

From a macro-cultural perspective, organizations adopt policies and practices oriented toward or away from cultural competence. On an individual or micro-cultural level, representatives of an agency enact the values and viewpoints of that particular organization.

Cultural Destructiveness

According to Mason et al. (1996), cultural destructiveness is the stage at which individuals and groups refuse to acknowledge the presence or importance of cultural differences in the teaching/ learning process. In addition, any perceived or real differences from dominant mainstream culture are punished and suppressed.

Institutions and individuals in this stage tend to endorse the myth of universality, insisting that all children conform to a mainstream middle class imperative. Given this stage, diverse learners are usually expected to shed any remains of their culture of origin in favor of the values and viewpoints of the dominant culture. Ordinarily, departures from this imperative are interpreted as deviant, deficient, or inferior. This orientation refuses to consider that schools must respond to children within a particular cultural context. Assumptions endorsed during the cultural destructiveness stage contribute to:

- Disenfranchised and disengaged learners
- Diminished levels of motivation
- Oppositional orientations towards education
- Premature departure from school
- Subsequent school failure

Educators operating in this stage often hold values, viewpoints, and orientations towards education that are contrary to what is considered standard or normative in the educational system of this country. Frequently, in this stage, organizations institute polices that penalize individuals and groups for their seeming differences.

Cultural Incapacity

Cultural incapacity refers to the stage in which cultural differences are neither punished nor supported. This occurs when the individual or organization chooses to ignore differences. Here, no attention, time, teaching, or resources are devoted to understanding and supporting cultural differences. Often educators and institutions remain oblivious to the relative importance of cultural competence. More attention may be devoted to curricular issues or to other priorities in the school, without considerations of cultural issues embedded in the curriculum. Educators may remain preoccupied with students' cognitive growth and maturity to the exclusion of their social, emotional, and cultural needs. During this stage, limited efforts are made to capitalize on the rich cultural resources children bring to school. Ironically, current understandings of cognitive development assume that learners integrate new information and materials with their existing constructions of the phenomena under consideration. It seems reasonable, therefore, that educators would maximize learning by incorporating cultural information into students' curricular experiences

Cultural Blindness

Cultural blindness represents the stage when the individual or organization actively proffers the notion that cultural differences are inconsequential and, as such, of no importance. Cultural differences may be noted but being color-blind (and culture-blind) is the desired state. No resources, attention, time, or teaching are devoted to understanding cultural differences. Often educators and institutions functioning in the color-blind stage construct their understanding of students from culturally different backgrounds using a race or cultural neutral lens.

Although some liberally minded individuals see this approach as a superior criterion for appearing bias-free, such a strategy often denies children an important aspect of their identity. Messages are communicated to students both overtly and covertly that their:

- Culture is of little consequence to their learning experience;
- Members of their ethnic group have made few meaningful contributions to society; and
- Cultural experiences are not legitimate in academic settings.

This severely inhibits students' levels of individual and collective effectiveness, often leads to an internalization of negative attitudes about the self and the cultural group, and contributes to the development of an oppositional orientation toward education described by Ogbu (1985). Whereas the first three stages demonstrate a certain indifference to the significance of cultural competence in maximizing learning outcomes for children from historically marginalized groups, the following two stages illustrate a conscious shift and openness towards addressing cultural differences.

Cultural Pre-competence

During *cultural pre-competence* stage, teachers, learners, and organizations recognize and respond to cultural differences and attempt to correct non liberating and unethical structures, teaching practices, and inequities. Openly acknowledging the need for cultural competency is an initial step toward destroying some of the debilitating practices that limit the educational progress of culturally diverse learners. Educators and school systems functioning at this stage may seek out new information about diversity by attending training sessions and/or interacting with individuals who have insider cultural information.

Cultural Competence

Finally, *cultural competence* is at the opposite extreme of the cultural destructiveness stage, wherein organizations and individuals learn to value cultural differences and attempt to find ways to celebrate, encourage, and respond to differences within and among themselves. Teachers and students explore issues of equity, cultural history and knowledge, social justice, and privilege and power relations in our society, and they do so in naturally occurring and often subconscious ways. Past and present differences are considered crucially relevant to the future of our society and the priorities and values of the next generation.

When schools, teachers, and learners are culturally competent, the culture that children bring to school serves as a resource for educators, the children themselves, their families, and the entire society. The students' funds of knowledge that are culturally filtered are valued and affirmed in contrast to the experiences of many previous generations whose identities and cultures were often distorted, marginalized, or even brutalized. As educators consider the sociopolitical issues that impact students' lives, as well as the cultural areas in this stage, there is a commitment to initiating structural changes that will positively impact the lives and educational experiences of learners from culturally distinct groups, as well as others.

Pedersen's Conceptual Framework for Developing Cultural and Cross-Cultural Competence

Pedersen (1994) developed a tripartite developmental model to promote cultural and multicultural understanding among practitioners. These competencies include the domains of:

- Awareness
- Knowledge
- Skills

Each domain builds successively on the previous one, such that mastery of an earlier domain is necessary before proceeding to subsequent domains. The awareness domain competency involves recognition of one's own biases as well as awareness of the sociopolitical issues that confront culturally different youngsters. Competencies in the knowledge domain involve the acquisition of factual information about different cultural groups. Finally, competencies in the skills domain involve integrating competencies in the previous awareness and knowledge domains in an effort to positively impact culturally distinct children.

Awareness domain competencies

Pedersen's (1994) conception of awareness competencies contains two overarching and significant issues. The first involves an individual's willingness to confront her or his own attitudes, values, and biases that may influence the pedagogical process. This notion is somewhat discussed in the section that deals with self-assessment. Achieving awareness competencies requires individuals to examine critically and analytically the following:

- How they obtained their attitudes and biases;
- How these biases impact the children they serve; and
- More importantly, how they can eliminate those biases.

If one does not confront these issues, mastering the next domain along Pedersen's continuum, i.e., knowledge, is difficult because each domain is predicated on successful completion of the previous domain.

A second issue identified in Pedersen's awareness model of cultural competence relates to an awareness of sociopolitical factors that confront culturally different groups. Several of these constructs facilitate our continued discussion of cultural competence and serve as the foundation for deep cultural understanding.

References

Mason, J. L., Benjamin, M. P., & Lewis, S. A. (1996). The cultural competence model: Implications for child and family mental health services. In C. A. Heflinger & C. T. Nixon (Eds.), Families and the mental health system for children and adolescents: Policy, services, and research. Children's mental health services (165-190). Thousand Oaks, CA: SAGE.

Ogbu, J. U. (1985). Research currents: Cultural-ecological influences on minority school learning. Language Arts, 62(8), 860-869.

Pedersen, P. (1994). A handbook for developing multicultural awareness. (2nd ed.). Alexandria, VA: American Counseling Association.

Sue, D. W., & Sue, D. (2003). Counseling the culturally diverse: Theory and practice. (4th ed.). New York: John Wiley & Sons.

CHAPTER 5
UNDERSTANDING YOUR WORLDVIEW

Understanding Your Own Worldview

A discussion of worldview provides a helpful framework for understanding how different cultural groups make sense of and interpret their experiences and worlds, including schooling and the educational process. As culturally competent educators, we must recognize and accept the reality that various cultural groups have vastly different fundamental beliefs and philosophical orientations. Worldviews consist of one's attitudes, values, opinions, concepts, thought and decision-making processes, as well as how one behaves and defines events (Sue & Sue, 1999) As an example, in traditional, dominant mainstream American culture, a family who has twins would define the first-born child as the older twin. In some West African cultures, the second-born twin is regarded as the elder twin.

The rationale for this African worldview lies in the belief that the second-born has a longer gestation period. Moreover, the second-born twin sends the first-born out into the world to assess the readiness of the environment so that the second-born twin may make her or his entry into the world. As we examine these two viewpoints, we must be mindful that neither perspective is wrong interpretations differ from each other. To place a value judgment on one belief over the other would be to invalidate a particular cultural group's conception of the world or its worldview

Understand various cultural worldviews

We must make two distinctions when we attempt to understand others worldviews. First, a Western cultural orientation refers more generally to people of various European ancestries and usually approximates a White, middle-class norm. A non-Western cultural orientation often refers to culturally distinct groups of African, Asian, Latino, and Indian ancestry. Although there are many distinctions within and between non-Western groups, at deep cultural levels, they share some very broad characteristics. See Table below

TABLE 1

Worldview	
Western Cultural Orientation	Non-Western Cultural Orientation
Individualism	Collectivism, Unity
Nuclear Family Structure	Extended Family Structure
Relationship – Hierarchical	Relationships – Collateral
Competition	Interdependence
Mastery over Nature	Harmony with Nature
Future Time Orientation	Present Time Orientation
Religion – Fragmented	Spirituality
Scientific Model	Intuitive Sense of Knowing
Communication – Verbal	Communication – Nonverbal

One's worldview is learned through socialization, from childhood to adulthood, and constantly reinforced by the culture in which we live. It is the taken- for-granted view of "the way things are" and most of the time unquestioned and invisible.

As reflected in Table 1, Western society, as previously discussed, tends to value individuals and individualistic orientations and values. The goal for educating children, given this view, generally is to produce independent and autonomous. In contrast, many non-Western cultures endorse worldviews and behaviors that consider the primal importance of the group over individual interests. In many groups, putting the individual or self before the collective is considered selfish and ill suited. We must weigh this cultural value in a relative context, particularly as it has an impact on children in educational settings. Within mainstream American culture the "model" nuclear family generally consists of two heterosexual parents and their offspring. Among many non-Western cultures, however, nonrelatives become part of the extended family network. African Americans, for example, may refer to nonrelatives who are closely involved with the family as aunts and uncles, often as fictive relatives. Similarly, many immigrant.

Latinos interact primarily with extended family members, siblings, cousins, and in-laws (Valdes, 1996). The extended family is paramount among Latinos in that it provides social support and wields considerable influence over family members. Among recently arrived immigrants, children are expected to grow up, work hard, live near home, and retain close involvement with the family (Valdes, 1996). Family loyalty is an important cultural value exemplified in this culture. Often, this loyalty is demonstrated by the proximity in which family members live to one another. Close family networks, however, may not encourage individual achievement and geographic mobility.

Competition is a value approved of in many Western cultures and is particularly apparent when considering the fact that capitalism is an integral part of American society. In schools, students generally compete for grades, status, academic and athletic performance. By contrast, many non-Western cultures emphasize the collective, which reduces the propensity for competition and individual performance. Consequently, a heavy regard is placed on the mutual interdependence of groups.

What is your worldview?

One Western worldview is "I am the captain of my soul," which is in contrast to the worldview of "God will provide" which other cultures hold. When one is blind to his own culture, he will not be able to see the differences in values between cultures. This could lead to cultural destructiveness, cultural imposition and cultural pain. This stems from cultural ignorance of one's own and other's cultural identities, due to intentional or unintentional isolation or separation. This leads to dehumanizing others with different values than one's own.

Competition is a value approved of in many Western cultures and is particularly apparent when considering the fact that capitalism is an integral part of American society. In schools, students generally compete for grades, status, academic and athletic performance. By contrast, many non-Western cultures emphasize the collective, which reduces the propensity for competition and individual performance. Consequently, a heavy regard is placed on the mutual interdependence of groups. Western cultural orientation uses the scientific model, which emphasizes acquisition of knowledge, results from testing scientific principles, and replicating investigations to ensure consistency over time. In many non-Western cultures people value and have an intuitive sense of knowledge obtained from personal and collective experiences, observations over time, and a collective wisdom. A thorough understanding of variations in worldviews helps to shed light on orientations that culturally different groups may have toward education.

Understanding Culture

We make assumptions about what each of us understands about "culture" and "cultural competence"; perhaps we should start by sharing aspects of our own "culture" with each other and with the children?'

- How might our views of culture affect our relationships with the students we serve?

- Does our environment reflect a genuine knowledge about the cultures of the students we serve?

Personal Reflection

You have a cultural, ethnic, and/or racial identity that shapes your understanding of the world, and your perceptions about others.

EXERCISE: Take a few minutes to write down your own cultural identity, and your experience of it.

Do you have a racial identity? How does it shape your view of yourself? After you have done this, discuss it with someone of a different culture or race.

_____
_____
_____
_____
_____
_____
_____
_____
_____
_____
_____
_____
_____
_____
_____
_____
_____
_____
_____
_____
_____
_____

REFLECTION

Recall and reflect on your earliest and most significant experiences of race, culture, and difference;

EXERCISE: HOW DO YOU VIEW THE FOLLOWING?

Aspects of Worldview	WHAT IS YOUR WORLDVIEW?
Time	
Space between you and the next	
Relationships	
Technology	
Religion or spirituality	
Honesty	

References

LeBaron, M. (2003). Bridging cultural conflicts: a new approach for a changing world. San Francisco, CA: Wiley.

Sue, D. W., & Sue, D. (2003). Counseling the culturally diverse: Theory and practice. (4th ed.). New York: John Wiley & Sons.

Valdes, G. (1996). Con respeto. Bridging the distances between culturally diverse families and schools. An ethnographic portrait. New York: Teachers College Press.

CHAPTER 6
RACIAL IDENTITY MODELS

Exercise: Answer the following questions:

1. What racial group do you identify with?

2. What ethnic group(s) do you identify with?

3. What socioeconomic class do you identify with?

4. What is your earliest memory of belonging in a group (other than your family)?

5. What is your earliest memory of being excluded from a group?

_____
_____
_____
_____
_____

6. What is your earliest memory of excluding someone from a group?

_____
_____
_____
_____
_____

Black Racial Identity

Several theories have been proposed to describe racial identity models for various racial and ethnic groups. In the following we will look at models for Black racial identity (Cross, 1991), White racial identity (Helms, 1984), as well as racial identities of culturally different and European groups (Sue & Sue, 1999). Racial identity theory pertains to the degree and quality of identification that individuals maintain toward those with whom they share common racial designations (Helms, 1993a) More specifically, it defines one's sense of affiliation or disassociation with others who possess the same racial heritage. Racial identity theories help people consider the heterogeneity of other individuals. That is, although people may share common racial designations, they may have distinct perceptions and attitudes about their own or others' racial designations. In short, these models help us avoid the tendency to view people as monolithic entities.

Cross's racial identity development model

Cross (1991) articulated four distinct stages of racial identity that explain the vast heterogeneity or within-group differences that characterize African Americans. They are as follows:

- Pre-encounter
- Encounter
- Immersion-emersion
- Internalization

In this paradigm, individuals transition from Eurocentric derivations of Blackness, which denigrate Black people, and gradually come to self-prescribed conceptualizations of Blackness, which esteem African-American worldviews, and value orientations, as well as other cultural orientations.

Pre-Encounter Stage

During the pre-encounter stage, individuals assume an assimilationist posture, devalue Blackness, and endorse Eurocentric notions of Blackness. Cross (1991) maintained that pre encounter individuals can assume a variety of orientations, which account for attitudes toward their ascribed racial group. For instance, some pre-encounter individuals have low-salience attitudes whereby they assign little or limited relevance to being African American.

Under such circumstances, these individuals grant higher priority to their religion, occupation, social class, or other distinctive status, and, consequently, de-emphasize their racial identity. Other pre-encounter individuals may possess social-stigma attitudes so that they perceive Blackness as an inconvenience or encumbrance. Still some pre-encounter individuals harbor anti-Black attitudes, such that they view other Blacks with disdain or contempt. This anti-black orientation usually results from miseducation and racial self-hatred (Vandiver, 2001).

Encounter Stage

The pre-encounter phase draws to a close once the individual experiences a catalytic or jolting event that causes her or him to reconstruct race more meaningfully. Cross argued consistently that the catalytic event is a necessary, yet not sufficient, condition for movement into the second stage, which is encounter. Not only must the individual experience a catalytic event or degrading experience during the encounter stage, she or he must also internalize such an event or experience by challenging pre-encounter viewpoints. Catalytic events include, but are not limited to, racial slights and indignities. Positive experiences such as exposure to a new aspect of African or African-American culture can also serve as the basis for reframing stereotypical derivations of race. During the encounter stage, individuals experience cognitive dissonance as a result of vacillating between two identity states, the previous identity and the emerging identity. Consequently, during the encounter stage, individuals pledge to begin an active search for their identity (White & Parham, 1990).

Immersion-Emersion Stage

During stage three, immersion-emersion, individuals bask in their newfound Black identities. Typically, stage-three individuals subscribe to externally driven dictates of what constitutes Blackness. "Ostentatious displays" of racial pride predominate this stage, such as adherence to Black norms of speech, dress, and social activity without internalizing this behavior. Immersion-emersion individuals direct overt hostility toward Whites in particular, or they may exhibit intense Black involvement such that they idealize all that is Black (Vandiver, 2001).

These angry emotions may include:

- Rage at Whites for having promulgated stereotypic notions of Blackness;

- A personal sense of shame and guilt for having previously denied Black racial identity; a

- Feelings of overwhelming pride which result from new levels of awareness and consciousness.

During the latter phase of this stage individuals emerge from this identity state with less idealistic and more objective views of Blackness

Internalization Stage

Finally, during stage four, internalization, African Americans demonstrate a greater sense of personal comfort and do not feel the overwhelming anger and hostility characteristic of the immersion-emersion stage. Given their more inclusive worldview, adolescents at this stage prescribe for themselves acceptable notions of Blackness and have a healthy appreciation towards members of their own racial group as well as acceptance of those with other racial and cultural backgrounds. Cross (1991) described three internalization identity types:

☐ Nationalist

☐ Biculturalist

☐ Multiculturalist

Distinguishing features of each involve the salience of one's Black identity in relationship to other dimensions of the identity structure. For instance, Black identity is the primary area of interest for nationalists, who devote their attention to the Black community. Biculturalists integrate their Black identity with a mainstream American identity. In addition to their racial identities, multiculturalists engage at least two other aspects of their identities, which may include gender, religion, or sexual orientation. They also demonstrate interest in issues pertaining to other racial groups (Vandiver, 2001). Table 2 summarizes Cross's model.

Table 2

Cross' Racial Identity Development Model

Pre-Encounter	Person devalues Blackness and endorses Eurocentric notions of Blackness.
Encounter	Person experiences a catalytic event that causes reconstruction of issues of race and ethnicity.
Immersion-Emersion	Person basks in newfound Black identity and idealizes everything that is Black
Internalization	Person achieves a more balanced appreciation of both Blacks and Whites

Parham (2000) revised Cross' 1991 model of psychological nigrescence, pointing out that racial identity development does not always follow a linear progression through the stages. What more likely results, notes Parham, is that individuals confront encounters or catalytic events periodically throughout their lifespan, which prompt them to recycle through encounter, immersion-emersion, and internalization stages.

White Racial Identity Development Model

Helms (1984) devised the white racial identity development (WRID) model in an effort to describe the transformations that occur among Whites as they transition from having negative attitudes about people of color to the adoption of a nonracist identity.

Helms proposed six statuses, which include:

1. Contact
2. Disintegration
3. Reintegration

4. Pseudo-independence

5. Immersion/emersion

During the *contact status,* Whites are generally oblivious to issues of racism and often adopt a color-blind perspective. In this stage people often vacillate between two extremes: they either have an uncritical acceptance of White racism, or they regard racial differences as unimportant. Endorsing the attitude that race is unimportant permits individuals to see themselves as members of the dominant group or as individuals with stereotypes.

During the *disintegration status*, individuals experience some conflict, which results from contradictions in their beliefs. For instance, parents may regard themselves as nonracist, yet forbid their children to play with children of color in the neighborhood. The irony in these viewpoints leads to feelings of shame and guilt. In an effort to resolve this dilemma, individuals may avoid contact with people of color, avoid thinking about issues of race, or maintain that they are not culpable for their attitudes.

During the *reintegration status*, the individual regresses, such that he or she returns to initial attitudes and behaviors. In this sense the individual once again idealizes Whiteness and shows indifference and contempt towards people of color.

During the *pseudo-independence status,* individuals continue to work towards adopting a nonracist identity. The person has difficulty accepting racism and may even begin to identify with people of color. Often people in this status make a conscious effort to interact with people from different racial and cultural groups. Ironically, while attempting to help people of color, Whites in this stage may inadvertently impose dominant values and viewpoints on minority groups.

Consequently, understanding during the pseudo-independence status occurs more at an intellectual level. People in the *immersion/emersion status* begin to ask what it means to be White. They want to understand the meaning of racism and how they have profited from white privilege (McIntosh, 1989). In this status people move from trying to change people of color to the development of an affective understanding. Many Whites during this status experience this honest appraisal of whiteness as redeeming and recuperative.

During the *final autonomy status,* individuals reduce their feelings of guilt and begin to accept their role in the perpetuation of racism. They value diversity and are no longer fearful or intimidated by issues of race and representation. People in this status develop a nonracist identity. Table 3 summarizes Helms' white racial identity developmental model.

Table 3

Helms' White Racial Identity Development Model

Status Description

Contact	Oblivious of own racial identity.
Disintegration	Conflict over contradictions between beliefs and behaviors.
Reintegration	Retreat to previous attitudes about superiority of Whites and the inferiority of people of color.
Pseudo-Independence	Intellectualized acceptance of own and others' race.
Immersion/Emersion	Honest appraisal of racism and significance of Whiteness.
Autonomy	Internalization of a multicultural identity with nonracist Whiteness as its core.

Sue and Sue's Racial/Cultural Identity Development Model

Sue and Sue (1999) identified five stages of racial identity development, which provide a useful synthesis of the attitudes and behaviors of people of color:

1. Conformity

2. Dissonance

3. Resistance and immersion

4. Introspection

5. Integrative awareness

During the *conformity stage* of this model, people of color have a preference for the dominant culture and tend to have negative impressions of people within their own racial and cultural groups. They may harbor feelings of shame and embarrassment about their racial or cultural group.

During the *dissonance stage*, individuals accumulate information and experiences that counter some of their conformity attitudes and beliefs. This newly acquired information creates a sense of cognitive dissonance for people of color as they confront issues of racism and oppression. For many, the dissonance stage is the first time they actually consider positive aspects of their racial or cultural group. Concurrently, viewpoints that question the superiority of the dominant culture begin to surface. Individuals functioning in the *resistance and immersion stage* tend to reject White social and cultural norms in favor of minority-held viewpoints.

During this stage individuals experience competing emotions–guilt, shame and anger–at having previously endorsed dominant cultural viewpoints, as well as pride in their new appreciation of their own race. Individuals in this stage feel a strong sense of connection to their own racial group.

During the *introspection stage,* individuals recognize that maintaining a strong orientation towards their own culture and an oppositional orientation towards the dominant culture is psychologically taxing. In addition, they realize that, despite their affinity to their own cultural group, they may not endorse all minority-held viewpoints. Strict adherence to minority-held viewpoints often requires that the individual subordinate her/his own autonomy. During this stage the individual may experience some conflict as he/she begins to recognize that not all aspects of American culture are bad. Individuals functioning in the integrative awareness stage develop a sense of inner security and have a healthy appreciation of their own culture as well as that of other people. Elements of this model are summarized in Table 4

Table 4

Sue & Sue's Racial/Cultural Identity Development Stages

Conformity	Oblivious of own racial identity.
Dissonance	Person challenges previously held beliefs and attitudes.
Resistance and Immersion	Person endorses minority held views and rejects dominant values of society and culture.
Introspection	Person recognizes unhealthiness of resistance and immersion stage
Integrative Awareness	Person has a balanced appreciation of own and others' culture.

Exercise: Level of Response

How do you relate to various groups of people in society? Please answer honestly, not as you think might be socially or professionally desirable.

Level of response:

1. I feel I can genuinely try to help this person without prejudice._____

2. Even though I do not agree with this person, I feel I can accept this person as he is and comfortable enough to listen to him/her._____

3. I do not feel that I have the background knowledge or experience to help this person._____

4. I feel uncomfortable taking care of this person._____

I feel biased and prejudiced against this person._____

Individual	Your Response
Iranian immigrant	
Child abuser	
Mexican American	
Elderly person with dementia	
Prostitute	
Methodist minister	
Gay/lesbian	
Unmarried expectant teen	
White Anglo-Saxon American	
Amputee	
Anorexic teenager	
Morbidly obese man in his 30s	
Norwegian	
Person with AIDS	
Person with cancer	
Person who does not speak English	

Exercise

Ethnocentrism is defined as the tendency of human beings to think that their ways of thinking, acting, believing are the only right, proper, and natural ways" and that beliefs, values and practices that differ from one's own are wrong. Unexplored assumptions about our biases and preconceived ideas about others will "blind" us to our ethnocentric behaviors and attitudes. Ethnocentrism is not an acceptable attitude in education because it deters from relationship building between the educator and the student.

Indicate the degree to which you agree to the following statements

1. People are responsible for their own actions.

   _____
   _____
   _____
   _____

2. The outcome of events is beyond our control.

   _____
   _____
   _____
   _____

3. It is dishonest to give vague and tentative answers

   _____
   _____
   _____
   _____

4. It is best to avoid direct and honest answers in order not to hurt or embarrass someone

5. Intelligent, efficient people use time wisely and are always punctual

6. Being punctual to work or meetings is not as important as spending time with family or close friends.

7. The best way to gain information is to ask direct questions.

8. It is rude and intrusive to ask direct questions.

9. It is proper to call people by their first names to show that you are friendly.

10. It is disrespectful to call people by their first names unless they give you permission.

10. It is rude not to look at a person who is speaking to you.

11. It is rude to engage in direct eye contact with persons of higher status.

References

Cross, W. E. (1991). Shades of Black: Diversity in African American identity. Philadelphia: Temple University Press.

Helms, J. E. (1984). Towards a theoretical explanation of effects of race on counseling: A black and white model. Counseling Psychologist, 12, 153-165.\

Helms, J. E. (1994a). Racial identity and career assessment. Journal of Career Assessment, 2, 199-209.

McIntosh, P. (1989, July/August). White privilege: Unpacking the invisible knapsack. Peace and Freedom, 10-12.

Sue, D. W., & Sue, D. (2003). Counseling the culturally diverse: Theory and practice. (4th ed.). New York: John Wiley & Sons.

Sue, D. W., & Sue, D. (1999). Counseling the culturally different: Theory & practice (3rd ed.). New York: Wiley.

Vandiver, B. J. (2001). Psychological nigrescence revisited: Introduction and overview. Journal of Multicultural Counseling and Development, 29, 165-173.

White, J. L., & Parham, T. A. (1990). The psychology of Blacks: An African-American perspective. Englewood Cliffs, NJ: Prentice-Hall.

CHAPTER 7
RACISM

Race and Racism

Nieto (1996) asserted that sociopolitical issues under gird our society and contended that any authentic attempt to promote an ethic of care and understanding using a cultural competency framework must address issues of oppression, racism, power, and privilege in schools. Others concur with her argument (Banks & Banks, 1997; Day Vines, 2000; Irvine & Irvine, 1995; Tatum, 1997). A critical component of addressing awareness competencies involves recognizing sociopolitical forces that impinge on individuals' lives. More specifically, oppression, racism, and powerlessness have schools operating as a microcosm of the larger society, such that students of color and students with disabilities experience the pernicious effects of oppression that frequently contribute to their orientation toward education and school outcomes. Racism is a particular form of oppression that refers to the systematic process of enlisting institutional resources, not only to support and promote a belief in the inferiority of groups on the basis of skin color but to deny opportunities to one group and subsequently grant them to a preferred group (Nieto, 1996; Tatum, 1997).

Reynolds and Pope (1991) defined oppression as "a system that allows access to the services, rewards, benefits, and privileges of society based on membership in a particular group." In general, "oppression" operates as an umbrella term that captures all forms of domination and control, including racism, sexism, heterosexism, and classism. Frequently people can experience single or even multiple forms of oppression. For instance, an African American female receiving special education services may experience:

1. Racism, as a representative of a culturally different group
2. Sexism, as a result of her gender
3. Linguicism, if she does not speak Standard English
4. An internalized sense of shame and embarrassment because of the stigma associated with a diagnosed learning disability

Educators working in a multicultural context must recognize that Scheurich and Young (1997) noted that many contend that, within popular culture, racism is often relegated to individual acts of meanness. They maintain, however, that racism cannot be reduced to forms of prejudice and discrimination that are enacted by an individual who feels a sense of entitlement and superiority over people from disadvantaged groups. Instead they propose that racism under girds numerous aspects of institutions, societies, and the world. Their work identified four categories of racism:

- Overt and Covert Racism
- Institutional Racism
- Societal Racism
- Civilizational Racism

Overt (Intentional) racism: An intentional and deliberate form of racism that is purposely enacted to inflict pain solely on the basis of race. Covert (Unintentional) racism lacks the planned calculation of overt racism, but results in similar consequences. For instance, a covert act of racism occurs when a child of color registers for class in a new school and it is assumed, on the basis of skin color and perhaps social class, that he or she requires a class for children with low abilities. In reality this child may have a stellar academic record and may even be eligible for gifted education service.

Institutional racism:

Refers to the establishment of institutionally sanctioned policies and practices that penalize members of a particular group on the basis of race, irrespective of the intentionality of such practices. Societal racism occurs when the social and cultural assumptions of one group are favored over the norms and dictates of another. For instance, the definition of a "model" nuclear family includes two heterosexual parents and their offspring(s). Deviations from this dominant cultural dictate are frequently regarded as an aberration and, consequently, devalued.

Societal racism

Occurs when the social and cultural assumptions of one group are favored over the norms and dictates of another. For instance, the definition of a "model" nuclear family includes two heterosexual parents and their offspring(s). Deviations from this dominant cultural dictate are frequently regarded as aberrations and, consequently, devalued.

Civilizational (Dysconscious) racism:

A broad construct that is deeply embedded in how people think. As our discussion of worldview demonstrated, different groups have vastly different orientations toward the world. Members within dominant groups or civilizations, however, often take the liberty of assigning a subordinate status to the values and viewpoints of groups regarded as lower in the societal hierarchy. The values and viewpoints of dominant groups often prevail as superior forms of functioning and, subsequently, become deeply embedded in the fabric of our society such that these views are seldom questioned. Such beliefs are embedded in many forms of scientific thought and often assume prevalence in popular culture and behavior. The most harmful aspect of racism is that it has an interlocking effect on minority groups and their experiences. Racism enacted at the civilizational level is supported and reinforced at lower levels. For instance, the mistaken belief that people of color are intellectually inferior has been promulgated at numerous levels. This has been most damaging in the scientific community, given the credence placed on such research in this society. Furthermore, data generated in the scientific community contribute to subsequent policies, practices, and individual behaviors.

Harmful aspects of Racism

The most harmful aspect of racism is that it has an interlocking effect on minority groups and their experiences. Racism enacted at the civilizational level is supported and reinforced at lower levels. For instance, the mistaken belief that people of color are intellectually inferior has been promulgated at numerous levels. This has

been most damaging in the scientific community, given the credence placed on such research in this society.

As an example, if the scientific community advances a theory of racial inferiority at the civilizational level, these beliefs give way to popular thought about the intellectual capacity of individuals at the societal level. Subsequently, institutional practices may follow that support the notion of:

- Racial inferiority such as incorporating the medical model of pathology versus incorporating the inherent strengths of particular groups;
- Tracking or assigning large numbers of minority children to special education;
- Assuming students for whom English is a second language should be classified for special education services;
- Not encouraging large numbers of students to attend college or enroll in college preparatory classes; and
- Maintaining low expectations for minority children.

On an individual level, both covert and overt forms of racism may occur that have the sanction of more complex forms of racism. A covert form of racism may involve the example provided above, wherein educators inadvertently assign a student to a class that does not meet her or his academic needs and abilities. An overt form of racism may occur when a teacher makes a disparaging comment about a student's racial group. An example described recently by a middle school child follows.

A Latina (female) child reported to a sixth-grade class in her new school toward the end of the school year, at which time the teacher gave her an assignment and explained that it was due in a week. Students in the class, however, had been given the assignment at the very beginning of the semester. When the time came for the child to submit the assignment, the student explained with some difficulty that she was not prepared.

Enraged, the teacher stated in the direct purview of all the children, that she fully expected her to submit assignments on time and she did not care whether her dog ate the homework or whether it falls on a hot tamale, (Day-Vines & Modest, 1998). This experience must have left the child feeling humiliated and devalued. The fact that the teacher made this comment with virtual impunity attests to the interlocking nature of multiple forms of racism that permit this behavior to occur unabated.

Acknowledging assumptions and biases

Culturally skilled individuals possess knowledge and understanding about how oppression, racism, discrimination, and stereotyping affect them personally and in their work. This allows them to acknowledge their own racist attitudes, beliefs, and feelings.

Employees are expected to be aware of their own cultural identifications in order to control their personal biases that interfere with the employee/client relationship.

Self-awareness involves not only examining one's culture, but also examining perceptions and assumptions about other's culture. Through a self-reflective assessment of their personal values, attitudes, and assumptions about other cultures, and articulating these assumptions and attitudes, individuals will gain the ability to sort out the influences of their own cultural background in order to provide respectful and unbiased services to others.

References

Banks, J. A., & Banks, C. A. (1997). Multicultural education: issues and perspectives. Hoboken, NJ: Wiley.

Day-Vines, Norma L. (2000). Ethics, Power, and Privilege: Salient Issues in the Development of Multicultural Competencies for Teachers Serving African American Children with Disabilities. Teacher Education and Special Education, 23(1), 3-18.

Irvine, J.J., & Irvine, R.W. (1995). Black students in schools: Institutional achievement and individual cultural perspectives: In R. L. Taylor (Ed.), Black youth: Their social and economic status in the U.S. Greenwood Press.

NIETO, S. (1996). Affirming diversity: the sociopolitical context of multicultural education. New York: Longman.

Reynolds, Amy L., & Pope, Raechele L. (1991). The Complexities of Diversity: Exploring Multiple Oppressions. Journal of Counseling & Development, 70(1), 174-180.

Scheurich, J. J., & Young, M. D. (1997). Coloring Epistemologies: Are Our Research Epistemologies Racially Biased? *Educational Researcher, 26*(4), 4. doi:10.2307/1176879

Tatum, B. D. (1997). *"Why are all the Black kids sitting together in the cafeteria?" and other conversations about the development of racial identity*. New York: BasicBooks.

CHAPTER 8
OPPRESSION

MATCHING GAME

1. Power   _____

2. Privilege   _____

3. Oppression   _____

4. Race   _____

5. Ethnicity   _____

6. Identity   _____

7. Gender   _____

8. Sexual Orientation _____

9. Class   _____

a. A social identity used interchangeably with biological sex in a system that presumes if one has male characteristics, one is male, and if one has female characteristics, one is female.

b. The system of ordering a society in which people are divided into sets based on perceived social or economic status.

c. A system that maintains advantage and disadvantage based on social group memberships and operates, intentionally and unintentionally, on individual, institutional, and cultural levels.

d. One's natural preference in sexual and/or romantic partners.

e. A category that describes membership to a group based on real or presumed common ancestry, shared languages and/or religious beliefs, cultural heritage and group history.

f. The sense of self, providing sameness and continuity in personality over time; the condition of being oneself and not another.

g. Unearned access to resources only readily available to some people as a result of their advantaged social group membership.

h. A socio-historical category used to divide people into populations or groups based on physical appearance, such as skin color, eye color, hair color, etc.

i. The ability to decide who will access to resources; the capacity to direct or influence the behavior of others, oneself, and/or the course of events.

FOCUSING INWARDS: ON SALIENT IDENTITIES

Take a few moments to think about your own identities. Which social groups do you belong to?

_____

_____

_____

Salient identities are the identities that come into play in different situations. Reflect on the following questions to yourself: Which of your social group memberships were easiest to identify?

_____

_____

_____

Which of your social group memberships were most difficult to identify?

_____

_____

_____

What questions are raised for you about your social group memberships?

_____

_____

Dynamics of Social Groups

Social statuses:

- Within each social identity category, some people have greater access to social power and privilege based on membership in their social group.

- Often, this group is called the advantaged group.

- We call group who access to social power is limited or denied, the targeted group.

- When you hear students or colleagues use the following terms in official paperwork or even in community conversation:

    Advantaged: agent, dominant, oppressor, privileged

    Targeted: target, subordinate, oppressed, disadvantaged

- **Social groups** are afforded different status in the United States based on multiple historical, political, and social factors.

    - This affects the abilities of people in different groups to access resources

    - Most of these differences and identities are socially constructed

        Social construction: taken for granted assumptions about the world, knowledge, and ourselves assumed to be universal rather than historically and culturally specific ideas created through social processes and interactions.

What does it mean to have power?

_____
_____
_____
_____
_____
_____

- When you hear that others feel as though they are "second-class citizens", what do you think that means?

_____
_____
_____
_____
_____

If you are feeling unempowered why might that be?

_____
_____
_____
_____
_____
_____

If your colleague feels unempowered, how can you support them?

_____
_____
_____
_____

What does a balance of power look like on campus?

___

Understanding Privilege

What does it mean to have privilege?

TALKING ABOUT PRIVILEGE

When talking about privilege, most folks feel uncomfortable. Having privilege is not inherently a bad thing, but it is how you utilize it and how others are impacted by it, that you must vigilantly attend to.

- What does privilege look like?

_____
_____
_____
_____
_____
_____

Can you think of examples of the following types of privilege?

- Class privilege _____
_____
_____

- White privilege _____
_____
_____
_____

- Heterosexual privilege _____
_____
_____
_____

- Able-bodied privilege _____
_____
_____
_____

- Religious privilege

- Citizenship privilege

- Name one action that can be done to provide access to those at your institution who may not have these privileges.

Understanding Oppression

Type of Oppression	Target Group	Non-Target Group
Racial	People of color	White people
Class	Poor; working class	Middle, owning class
Gender	Women	Men
Sexual orientation	Lesbian, gay, transgender, bisexual	Heterosexual people
Ability	People with disabilities	People without disabilities
Religion	Non-Christian	Christian
Elderly	**People over 40**	**Age**
Youth	Children and young adults	Older adults
Rank/status	People without college degree	People with college degree
Military service	Vietnam veterans	Veterans of other wars
Immigrant status	Immigrant	U.S.-born
Language	Non-English	English

Ways To Unravel Systemic Oppression

By viewing the film, *Fruitvale Station*, you could be taking one step towards creating a more just and equitable society. Educating ourselves is an important starting point in this effort, and here are some more actions you can take to unravel systemic oppression and its offspring, bias and prejudice.

1. Learn, learn, learn: Continue educating yourself about issues of systemic oppression. If you work in schools, it's essential to understand the school-to-prison pipeline, as that's a forceful reflection of systemic oppression. Start with reading Michelle Alexander's *The New Jim Crow: Mass Incarceration in the Age of Colorblindness.*

2. Discuss holistically: When discussing about other groups who have been oppressed, don't define those "others" by their oppression. There is more to being African American than slavery, more to being Jewish than the Holocaust; find those stories and representations that depict people in their full humanity and share those. Furthermore, go "beyond heroes and holidays" when discussing about other people. Mexican (and Mexican-American) history can be addressed at many points throughout the year, not just on Cinco de Mayo.

3. Analyze the data:? Ask yourself hard questions and look for patterns that reflect those found in our society of who succeeds and who is marginalized.

4. Teach holistically: When talking about other groups who have been oppressed, don't define those "others" by their oppression. There is more to being African American than slavery, more to being Jewish than the Holocaust; find those stories and representations that depict people in their full humanity and share those. Furthermore, go "beyond heroes and holidays" when talking about other people. Mexican (and Mexican-American) history can be addressed at many points throughout the year, not just on Cinco de Mayo.

5. Interrupt inequities: If you notice inequitable patterns in an area that you have some control or influence over, do something about it.

6. Get another perspective: Invite a trusted colleague to observe for the manifestation of any unconscious beliefs that might value one group over another. Ask your colleague to raise difficult questions about your interactions, to push you. We can't see our own blind spots.

7. Know yourself: Explore your own biases and consider how they might impact your decision-making. Racism is learned and we can unlearn it. We all have biases -- it's near impossible to not acquire some. As Beverly Tatum says, it's like smog in the air we breathe. Unlearning starts with uncovering what we might not want to look at.

8. Listen to Learn: Reach out to the students, parents, and colleagues who come from different backgrounds and experiences to your own. Don't ask them to teach you about who they are or "their people," instead, shorten that distance between you and look for ways to authentically connect, and listen to learn about who they are. Ask for their opinions and perspectives on your teaching, your curriculum, ways of engaging with students, and so on.

9. Interrupt unproductive dialogue: If you hear colleagues express views that stereotype other people or reduce their humanity, or if you hear colleagues say something that might reflect a pattern of systemic oppression, respond. You don't have to respond in the moment; you can take a time out and reflect, compose your thoughts and words, confer with someone else if necessary, and then return to speak with the person. But don't let things slide. If you get that gnawing feeling of, *I should have said something*, go back, and say, "Hey, a few weeks ago you said... Can we talk about that?"

10. **Manage your discomfort:** Talking about race, class, and privilege isn't easy. Know that it will be uncomfortable, and perhaps painful, and recognize that this discomfort also emerges from a system of oppression. Systems of oppression perpetuate by keeping many members of the system silent. Breaking that silence puts us one step closer to dismantling it.

In what ways do you break the silence with your colleagues and in your classroom?

_____
_____
_____
_____
_____
_____
_____
_____
_____
_____
_____

OPRESSION

Think about the role schools played in the dynamics of oppression when you were a young person.

1. Can you think of policies or practices that have negative consequences for members of a particular group?

_____
_____
_____
_____
_____
_____
_____

2. How was what happened in school supported in other institutions?

_____
_____
_____
_____
_____
_____

3. What strategies did communities, families, and individuals use to resist discrimination and organize on their own behalf

_____
_____
_____
_____
_____
_____

Oppression

Social Identity Cateories	Privileged Social Groups	Border Social Groups	Targeted Social Groups	Ism
Race	White People	Biracial People (White/Latino, Black, Asian?	Asian, Black, Latino, Native People	Racism
Sex	Bio Men	Transsexual Intersex People	Bio Woman	Sexism
Gender	Gender Conforming Bio Men And Women	Gender Ambiguous Bio Men and Women	Transgender, Genderqueer, Intersex Peoples	Transgender Oppression
Sexual Orientation	Heterosexual People	Bisexual People	Lesbian, Gay Men	Heterosexism
Class	Rich, Upper Class	Middle Class People	Working Class, Poor People	Classism
Ability/Disability	Temporarily Abled-Bodied People	People with Temporarily Disabilities	People with Disabilities	Ableism
Religion	Protestants	Roman Catholic (historically)	Jews, Muslims, Hindus,	Religious Oppression
Age	Adults	Young Adults	Elders, Young People	Ageism/Adultism

References

Alexander, M. (2016). *New jim crow: mass incarceration in the age of colorblindness.* Place of publication not identified: New Press.

CHAPTER 9

POWER AND PRIVILEGE

Privilege

Like a fish in water

Let's begin to think about concepts of power and privilege by considering a fish swimming in water. The fish has no awareness that it is in water because the water has always been there. The fish only notices the water when it is taken out of it, and then what it notices is the absence of the water, not its presence.

As human beings, we live in a world infused with power and privilege. We live in a culture where personal power often relates directly to levels of privilege. This privilege is based on societal attitudes and values over which individuals typically have no control. We often don't notice these aspects of our culture because we are immersed in them. In much the same way as with the fish, it is generally the absence of power and privilege that triggers our awareness, not the presence. Would any of the people in the image below be aware that they are privileged in some way? Are they completely unaware like the fish in the analogy?

Privilege defined

Privilege exists when one group has something of value that is denied to others simply because of the groups they belong to, rather than because of anything they have done or failed to do.*(Johnson, 2006, p. 21)*

Privilege is often granted to an individual or group based on who they are or what they represent in our culture rather than anything they have done. Similarly, those not among privileged groups are often faced with unique challenges again based on who they are rather than what they have done or failed to do.

Like the fish, we may not always be conscious of how our group memberships affect our privilege in every situation. These group memberships include, but are not limited to, class, gender, race and ethnicity, sexual orientation, gender identity, ability status, faith tradition, level of education, and age. Each of us is going to have some position and resulting level of privilege within each of these categories.

"Regardless of which group we're talking about, privilege generally allows people to assume a certain level of acceptance, inclusion, and respect in the world, to operate within a relatively wide comfort zone."*(Johnson, 2006, p. 32-33)*

As mentioned earlier, much of the privilege that exists in a culture is not obvious to all members of that society. Depending on your gender, race and ethnicity, class, sexual orientation and other identities, you might be more or less aware of privilege as well as who holds power in various aspects of the culture.

Take a moment to consider the following questions and consider your awareness of these realities and test your knowledge.

- Who has always held the presidency in the United States?

  _____
  _____

- Which categories of people have never held that office?

  _____
  _____

- Who is most often the victim of sexual assault?

  _____
  _____

- Who is more likely to be targeted by police officers for driving an expensive car in a wealthy neighborhood?

  _____
  _____

- Whose holidays do we most prominently celebrate?
  _____
  _____

- Which groups are targeted most for hate crimes?
  _____
  _____

- Who can and cannot get married in the U.S.? _____
  _____

If you are someone who sees themselves mirrored in the people who are privileged in this country, you are less likely to notice who is not included. If you do not face the reality of violence directed at you because of who you are or you do not have to attempt to hide who you are for safety, then you may not realize the effect this has on those who do. Not noticing these things is part of the luxury that privilege affords.

As noted above, the amount of privilege that a person has can influence many aspects of his or her life. Some of these aspects include career and employment mobility, personal safety issues, and the freedom to marry. In the next section we will further explore some of the ways personal power results from privilege.

When a group of college students were asked their ideas about privilege, they identified several themes including money, opportunities, discrimination, race, gender, merit, and power (Chizhik & Chizhik, 2002). Notably, the students saw power as an important aspect of privilege.

Power defined

Power is defined in Merriam Webster's as "the ability to act or produce an effect" as well as "a possession of control, authority, or influence over others." *(Merriam Webster's Collegiate Dictionary)*. Where privilege is granted to someone as a result of who they are and where they come from, the personal power to cause things to happen is often a result of that privilege. In order for an individual to cause something to happen or to make a change in a given situation, he or she must have the resources to do so. Individuals who have more societal approval and support, hence privilege, are going to be much more likely to hold positions of power in that society and able to make decisions that affect the lives of many people, including their own.

For example, someone from a very wealthy family will enjoy privileges associated with that wealth. These privileges may include access to quality schooling and healthcare, membership in country clubs, and the freedom to travel and vacation. A person with wealth may also choose to use that wealth to control the lives of other people or they may donate much of their money to charity and assume no control for how the money is spent. Because of their privilege, they have the choice of what they want with the money and this naturally gives them power in many situations.

Power is often understood in terms of familial and employment structures. For example, parents have power over their children because they can set rules and dole out consequences and rewards regarding those rules. Instructors have power over students because they give assignments and then grade students based on how they complete those assignments. Bosses have power over workers because they can hire or fire, promote or demote employees based on their perceptions of how they are doing.

Less obvious forms of power in our society result from privileges due to gender, race and ethnicity, sexuality, class, level of education and other attributes. For instance, as shown in the graphic below, we know that worldwide, approximately one in five women will be the victim of rape or attempted rape (UN Millennium Project, 2005). We also know that one in three will have been physically abused in some form, including beatings and the coercion to have sex (Heise, 1999).

We know that worldwide, approximately **one in five** women will be the victim of rape or attempted rape (UN Millenium Project, 2005). We also know that **one in three** will have been physically abused in some form, including beatings and the coercion to have sex (Heise, 1999).

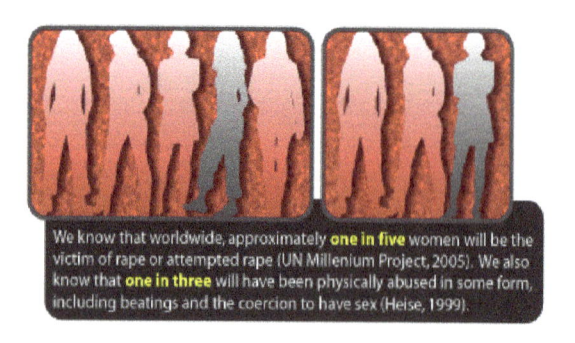

Because the vast majority of these assaults are committed by men, a male in our society has power over any woman based on the reality that a woman knows that she could be assaulted in many situations and that the perpetrator is likely to be male. A man may never assault or harm a woman, but the prevalence of violence against women by men automatically gives him power based on his gender. This gives a woman less power in a variety of situations because she may not feel able to exercise the same freedoms as a man based on fear of being assaulted. Freedom to feel comfortable going out alone after dark is only one example of this dynamic.

Exploring your Identity

As we further explore power and privilege, it is important to consider the ways in which we each experience the world through the things that give us our identity. Each of us has a gender, a race, an ability status, an ethnicity, a sexual orientation, a faith tradition, an age, a class status, and many other attributes that make up who we are. The following worksheet will help you explore these areas.

Please complete the following Social Group Membership Profile worksheet to refer to throughout the workshop.

Social Group Membership Profile Activity

For each of the following categories, identify your identity:

Gender: _____
Race: _____
Ethnicity: _____
Ability Status : _____
Sexual Orientation: _____
Religion: _____
Age: _____
Class: _____
Other: _____

Then consider the following questions based on the social group memberships you've identified above.

1. What memberships do you think of most often? Why?

   _____
   _____
   _____

2. What memberships do you consider least? Why do you think that is?

   _____
   _____
   _____

3. What memberships give you the most privileges? What are those privileges?

   _____
   _____
   _____
   _____

4. What memberships hurt your options or opportunities the most? How?

   _____
   _____
   _____
   _____

5. What memberships do you want to learn more about? Why?

   _____
   _____
   _____
   _____

6. What memberships make you the most comfortable? Why?

   _____
   _____
   _____
   _____

7. What memberships have the strongest effect on your self image and how?

_____
_____
_____
_____
_____

8. What membership plays a greater role in how others see you? How?

_____
_____
_____
_____
_____
_____
_____

EXERCISE: Exploring your Privilege

The following exercise will help you explore your own privilege in several areas. This can be difficult and you may find yourself feeling uncomfortable, defensive, or even angry. We encourage you to recognize those feelings and to continue with the exercise. By doing so, you will begin to discover more about privilege and the power that can come with it. You may begin to look critically at your own life and the society in which you live.

- You will start the exercise with $15 in your "privilege piggy bank."
- You will be given a series of questions to be answered "yes," "no," or "not sure" and after you answer each question, your privilege currency will increase, decrease, or stay the same.
- You will finish with between $0 and $30.
- There are no right or wrong answers, simply the answers that best fit your lived experience in each of these areas.
- Be sure to answer all 15 questions.

Discussion of Exploring your Privilege Exercise

As you worked on this exercise, you may have noticed that you had some strong feelings such as frustration, anger, or guilt. As stated at the beginning, there are no right or wrong answers to these questions and when you consider your final "privilege currency" amount, use it as a guide to think about those areas in your life where you have experienced more privilege and those areas where you have experienced less privilege. Privilege and the lack of it can affect our personal power, self-esteem, the choices we make about our education In reflecting on this exercise, think about the following questions:

- How did this exercise make you feel?

- Were your thoughts as you were doing it?
- What have you learned from this exercise?
- Where is there privilege on this campus? In your community? In the U.S.? In the world?

The exercise you have just completed is adapted from an interactive activity called "The Privilege Walk." We didn't use all of the questions, but chose questions that addressed the various forms privilege can take.

Race and Ethnicity, Gender, and Sexual Orientation

We have been looking broadly at the concepts of privilege and the ways in which power is a function of that privilege. For the next three sections, we will look specifically at power and privilege in the context of race and ethnicity, gender, and sexual orientation. These are only three examples among many. In examining these specific examples, consider how privilege and power also function in other areas like age, ability status, religious affiliation, size, and class.

Race, Ethnicity and Power and Privilege

Issues of race and ethnicity have been some of the more visible and historically significant aspects of privilege in this country. People of color have experienced some of the most powerful discrimination and resultant lack of privilege that our society has produced. Issues of slavery, segregation in education, and hate crimes are only some of the ways that power has been used to affect this underprivileged group of people. Skin color and ethnic background are some of the first things that many people notice about another person and this makes a person of color an easy target for any person who wishes to use power against him or her. Living with this reality is not something that those who are white can fully comprehend.

A Slave nurse holds her young master in this photo made about 1850. Slaves in America were charged with many responsibilities, including raising their masters' offspring who eventually learned to give orders and think of their surrogate mothers as property. (AP Photo/Missouri).

Students of Central High School in Little Rock, Ark., including Hazel Bryan, shout insults at Elizabeth Eckford as she calmly marches down to a line of National Guardsmen, who blocked the main entrance and would not let her enter, Sept. 4, 1957. (AP PHOTO/Arkansas Democrat Gazette/Will Counts)

The Keystone Knights of the Ku Klux Klan salute the burning crucifix at a cross burning just outside Chaneysville, Pa., on the Bedford County Farm of a woman Friday night, June 14, 1996. Yvonne Conrad had to be physically restrained by more than two dozen Ku Klux Klan members as she tried unsuccessfully to stop them from lighting the 18-foot cross on her farm. The rally was billed as a kickoff for the Keystone Knights' summer activities. (AP Photo/Tribune Review, Marc Fader)

I have come to see white privilege as an invisible package of unearned assets that I can count on cashing in every day, but about which I was 'meant' to remain oblivious. White privilege is like an invisible weightless knapsack of special provisions, assurances, tools, maps, guides, code books, passports, visas, clothes, compass, emergency gear, and blank checks.

(McIntosh, 1998, p. 94-95)

One of the interesting things that happens when we have privilege is that we can often see that those who don't have it are at a disadvantage (McIntosh, 1992). In terms of race and ethnicity, it is often easier for a white person to identify that persons of color have less privilege than it is to acknowledge the privileges of being white in our society. For example, if I am a white person, I may be able to identify that life is more difficult for people of color. However, because of what racism teaches all of us, I may believe that there is something about being a person of color that brings on the difficulties. It is not uncommon for a person to hold the belief that someone who is oppressed is somehow at fault for that lack of privilege.

Consider the following examples:

- If I notice that people of color seem more likely to be recipients of public assistance, I may believe that if they would only work harder, they would have enough money to have a better standard of living.
- If I read about a man of color who was arrested for driving his expensive car in a wealthy neighborhood, I may think that of course the police officers needed to be careful.
- I may notice that people of color are over represented in prison populations, and I may believe that this means that there is something about race that makes people more likely to commit crimes.

What we fail to acknowledge when we blame people for their own lack of privilege and the circumstances that result is the lack of power they have in many situations. If a person of color is discriminated against in housing, employment, or education based on the opinion and choices of someone with power in those situations, then it is hard for them to effect change in their situation. A person of color may be not welcome in certain businesses or may feel that they will be the target of suspicion if a crime occurs when they are living in a predominately white neighborhood. These are not the same realities that most white persons live with. The lack of choice that comes with having less privilege and therefore power is only compounded by the challenges faced in society.

Gender and Power and Privilege

Issues of gender and privilege have been a common theme in society for many years. The women's liberation movement in the 1960's and 1970's brought into focus some of the privileges that men enjoyed based on gender and how their use of power affected the lives of women. If we look closely at the social status of women and men, we can see that men continue to have privilege over women in many aspects of life. Only rarely will a man go beyond acknowledging that women are disadvantaged to acknowledging that men have unearned advantage, or that unearned privilege has not been good for men's development as human beings, or for society's development, or that privilege systems might ever be challenged and changed. *(McIntosh, 1998, p. 95)* . We must examine how this correlates with the power men hold in our society and over the lives of women. This is similar to the issue discussed in the race and ethnicity section regarding white privilege.

![Infographic showing wage comparison: White Men 100, White Women 75.5, African American Women 65.4, Hispanic Women 54.3. The ways that male privilege is evident in society are numerous. Consider that "White women's wages are now at about 75.5 cents for every dollar white men make, and Black or African American women earn 65.4 cents, Hispanic women earn 54.3 cents compared with that dollar. There is less of a wage gap between Black and Hispanic women and men: about 83-88 percent" (Ruby, 2005).]

The ways in which men hold privilege and therefore have access to power are often more evident to women than they are to men. For example, women are more likely to see domestic violence, workplace harassment, and wage discrimination as major barriers to their quality of life than men are.

Although a man might be aware of some of the issues facing women in our culture, he might attribute those challenges to her own character rather than the environment in which she is existing. Because women are immersed in a society where male points of view are the predominant focus, women may also hold similar views and blame women for their own oppression.

Consider the following examples:

- If I am a man, I may notice that women are most often victims of sexual assault. I may blame a woman for causing her assault and not focus on the choice that a man makes in assaulting a woman. I may also not be aware of how the reality of sexual assault affects the lives of women and their freedom.
- As a man, I can choose any career that I want to pursue and am less likely to face harassment or discrimination as a result. Women who choose careers in the military and other non-traditional fields often face discrimination that directly impacts their career success.

Much of the privilege and power that men have over women in our culture today is unearned power. To become truly aware about his power over others, a man must make an effort to educate himself about the ways in which women are underprivileged and more importantly, how he as a man has enjoyed unearned privilege based on his gender. As with other members of a privileged group, men have choice in raising their awareness about gender privilege while women are often very aware of it based on their lived experiences.

Sexual Orientation and Power and Privilege

Sexual orientation is one of the less visible aspects of a person and consequently we may not even know that someone we are interacting with is gay, lesbian, or bisexual. Because of the stigmas attached to having a sexual orientation that is other than heterosexual, many choose not to share their sexual identity in our culture. Along with fear for personal safety and discrimination in housing and employment, the fact that in some states same sex sexual activity is illegal keeps individuals in hiding.

In an effort to promote equality and safety, many men and women have taken the risk of becoming visible in order to gather together and increase their power to fight the discrimination that affects them in many ways. While issues of privilege are now more recognizable with regard to sexual orientation, heterosexual individuals may still be biased with regard to whether or not lesbians and gays deserve the rights and protections they are seeking. Because they have the power to shape public policy, these biased views can greatly compound the lack of privilege that exists. Consider some of the ways that a lesbian woman, gay man or bisexual person is affected by being in this underprivileged group:

- Heterosexuals can comfortably and safely talk about their relationships with opposite sex partners where gay men, lesbian women, and bisexual individuals often censor their discussions, choosing their pronouns carefully.
- Heterosexuals can easily work as teachers or with children in other capacities where many people still argue that children aren't safe with gay men or lesbian women because they are always looking for new "recruits."
- Heterosexuals can legally marry their opposite sex partners where gay or lesbian couples may live together but with few exceptions are not allowed to legally marry.

Assumptions about the normalcy of heterosexuality and the difference of homosexuality are so deeply ingrained that to look at heterosexuality the way society looks at homosexuality can be quite illuminating.

As an example, consider the following sample of questions from the **Heterosexual Questionnaire** (Rochlin, M., 1989).

- What do you think caused your heterosexuality?

- When and how did you first decide you were a heterosexual?

- Is it possible your heterosexuality is just a phase you may grow out of?

- Is it possible your heterosexuality stems from a neurotic fear of others of the same sex?

- If you have never slept with a person of the same sex, is it possible that all you need is a good gay lover?

- Do your parents know that you are straight? Do your friends and/or roommate(s) know? How did they react?

_____
_____
_____

- Why do you insist on flaunting your heterosexuality? Can't you just be who you are and keep it quiet?

_____
_____
_____

- Why do heterosexuals place so much emphasis on sex?

_____
_____
_____

Although we are unable to assess the number of gays, lesbians, and bisexual people in our culture due to their fear of being stigmatized, we must be conscious that there are probably people who have differing sexual orientations in our daily lives. It is up to each of us to be sensitive to this fact and the ways in which heterosexuals enjoy privilege over this population. When we think critically about this, the privilege is obvious and ranges from freedom to walk down the street holding hands without fear of violence to the ability to build a family with a long term partner.

Conclusion

Power and privilege are complex issues. As individuals, we see the world through the lens of our own values and lived experiences. College students have some privilege because of their education. Less than 28% of the people living in the U.S. over 25 have a college degree (U.S. Census Bureau, 2003). Part of being able to function as an aware and thoughtful citizen and of the world is developing the capacity to think about power and privilege and how they impact the people in a community.

It is often true that those groups in our culture who have less privilege will join together in groups in order to try and increase their collective power to influence cultural change. Additionally, all of us who have privilege can be allies for those who don't. As allies, we can use our power and privilege to speak up for equitable treatment and to speak out against bigotry and oppression. For example, if I am a man, I can address inequities that women experience. If I am white, I can address the inequities that people of color experience. If I am heterosexual, I can address the inequities that LGBT people experience. These are just some of the ways in which we can use our power and privilege in positive ways. It is important to realize that we benefit from the privilege we have, and it is equally important to acknowledge that we often benefit from the underprivileged status of others. It is up to each of us to make conscious choices about how we use our power and the effects it has on other people.

Social Group Membership Profile

For each of the following categories, identify your identity:

Gender: _____
Race: _____
Ethnicity: _____
Ability Status: _____
Sexual Orientation: _____
Religion: _____
Age: _____
Class: _____
Other: _____

Then consider the following questions based on the social group memberships you've identified above.

1. What memberships do you think of most often?

    _____
    _____
    _____
    _____
    _____
    _____

2. Why? _____

    _____
    _____
    _____
    _____
    _____

3. What memberships do you consider least?

    _____
    _____
    _____
    _____
    _____
    _____

4. Why do you think that is?

    _____
    _____
    _____
    _____

5. What memberships give you the most privileges?

6. What are those privileges?

7. What memberships hurt your options or opportunities the most?

8. How?

9. What memberships do you want to learn more about?

10. Why?

11. What memberships make you the most comfortable?

12. Why?

13. What memberships have the strongest effect on your self image and how?

14. What membership plays a greater role in how others see you?

15. How?

Recognizing and Responding to Power and Privilege as a Form of Cultural Competency

Pinderhughes (1989) identified the function of power and powerlessness when individuals from different racial and cultural groups interact. Educators from dominant cultural groups wield power, both individually and institutionally, and influence both as members of an esteemed group and as authority figures in the classroom. In striking contrast, learners with disabilities may feel powerless and vulnerable as members of devalued groups. Ethical practice requires that teachers remain cognizant of power dynamics both in the classroom and in society and work to consciously eliminate the arrangements that jeopardize student learning.

Power

Power is a sociopolitical process that effects change and wields influence over others, especially in a manner that diminishes one's own sense of personhood (Pinderhughes, 1989) Powerlessness, on the other hand, functions as the corollary to power and refers to the inability of a person to effect change and influence the outcomes in her or his life (Sue & Sue, 1999) (Activity 2.8). This occurs particularly under circumstances in which status differentials exist between an individual with more power and one with less power. An examination of some values associated with mainstream American culture reveals a number of power dynamics. Embedded in the values of individualism, personal mastery, competition, and acquisition of material goods are notions that individuals must exercise control, dominion and authority over themselves and others. Although power can be exercised in a manner that is just and equitable, too frequently power is abused so that individuals with less power are manipulated, controlled, and coerced. As an example, the common practice of tracking has been described as an institutional practice that severely limits the educational opportunities for students whose cultures, language, and socioeconomic status differ from those in the dominant American culture (Robinson & Howard- Hamilton, 2000). Power can also be used for self-enhancement to reinforce another individual's sense of powerlessness and inadequacy.

This form of power is often manifested through establishing a form of paternalistic responsibility to others. Further, responses to powerlessness by children and youth may include aggression, disruptive behavior, resentment, and also internalized shame (Pinderhughes, 1989). Students from marginalized groups may internalize a sense of powerlessness on more than one level. They may feel a sense of powerlessness with respect to issues of race, gender, social class, disability, and sexual orientation.

Privilege

McIntosh (1989) provided a candid discussion of "white privilege" as an obligatory dimension of racism, which provides dominant learners with decided social, cultural, political, economic, and educational advantages relative to marginalized learners. Privilege grants a set of benefits and system rewards to one group while simultaneously excluding other groups from accessing these advantages.

Additionally, McIntosh defined white privilege as "an invisible weightless knapsack of special provisions, assurances, tools, maps, guides, codebooks, passports, visas, clothes, emergency gear and blank checks". More notably, she acknowledged that systems of dominance remain firmly entrenched in our society because beneficiaries of "white privilege" remain perpetually in a state of denial and repression about their advantages.

One example of such privilege is that white shoppers are not followed around in stores with someone assuming they are there to steal. In the context of education, white privilege, or the protective mechanism of skin color, often predisposes middle-class Caucasian children to:

- Fewer discipline referrals
- Reduced likelihood of being falsely identified as having disabilities
- More recommendations for gifted and talented programs
- Advanced and college-bound classes
- More preferential treatment by teachers
- Greater recognition for accomplishments

In some instances, the beneficiaries of white privilege avoid penalties and in other instances privilege confers a questionable sense of meritocracy on its beneficiaries. These privileges and systems of dominance are seldom acknowledged but continuously place students who meet a White middle-class imperative at an advantage while penalizing students from marginalized groups. McIntosh would argue that maintenance of this system of privilege relies on an unwillingness to confront these social realities and the necessity of pretending in order to reinforce it.

Educators must lay bare the system of privilege if authentic and meaningful structural elements of cultural competency are to be achieved. As discussed elsewhere in this document, an educator who endorses cultural competency **practice has an ethical responsibility to work** diligently to preserve the dignity and human worth of all students and create a learning environment that empowers children and adolescents.

Understanding one's own attitudes, feelings, and behaviors is a prerequisite for extending an ethic of care to students from marginalized groups. Moreover, this understanding contributes to the development of cultural competence. Authentic multicultural understanding also results from honestly recognizing and confronting the sociopolitical realities that impact the lived experiences of people of color in this country.

Knowledge of Pedersen's awareness stage contributes significantly to the likelihood that educators will use their personal power to effect change and engage in social action and ethical practice on behalf of powerless groups or remain silent and complicit.

Becoming aware of one's own biases as well as recognizing sociopolitical issues such as oppression, racism, power, and privilege function as initial strategies that naturally lead into the **cultural competence sequence.**

References

American Civil Liberties Union. (n.d.). Racial Profiling: Old and New. Retrieved January 23, 2006, from http://www.aclu.org/racialjustice/racialprofiling/index.html

Andrews, M., Carlson, S., & Nord M. (2004). Household Food Security in the United States, 2003. *ERS Research Brief.* Retrieved January 23, 2006, from http://www.ers.usda.gov/publications/fanrr42/fanrr42_researchbrief.pdf

Business and Professional Women's Foundation. (2005). *101 Facts on the Status of Workingwomen.* Retrieved January 23, 2006, from http://www.bpwusa.org/files/public/101FactsonWorkingwomen2005.pdf

Chizhik, E. W., & Chizhik, A. W. (2002). Decoding the language of social justice: What do privilege and oppression really mean? *Journal of College Student Development,* 43(6), 792-80

Fears, D. (2003, June 20). Hue and cry on 'Whiteness Studies.' *The Washington Post*, p. A01. Retrieved January 24, 2006 from http://www.washingtonpost.com/ac2/wp-dyn/A14386-2003Jun19?language=printer

Heise, L., Ellsberg, M. and Gottemoeller, M. (1999). Ending violence against women. Population Reports. Retrieved January 24, 2006, from http://www.infoforhealth.org/pr/l11edsum.shtml

Johnson, A. (2006). *Privilege, power, and difference*. New York: McGraw-Hill.

Joyce, A. (2005, December 9). The Bias Breakdown. *The Washington Post,* p. D01. Retrieved December 9, 2005, from http://www.washingtonpost.com/wp-dyn/content/article/2005/12/08/AR2005120802037.html

McIntosh, P. (1998). White privilege and male privilege: A personal Account of coming to see correspondences through work in women's studies. In M.L. Andersen & P.H. Collins (Eds.), *Race, class and gender* (pp. 94-105). Belmont, CA: Wadsworth Publishing Company.

Merriam-Webster's Collegiate Dictionary. (10th ed.). (1993). Springfield, MA: Merriam Webster.

National Mental Health Association. *Bullying in schools: Harassment puts gay students at risk*. Retrieved January 19, 2006, from http://www.nmha.org/pbedu/backtoschool/bullyingGayYouth.pdf

Pinderhughes, E. (1989). Understanding race, ethnicity, and power: The key to efficacy in clinical practice. New York: Free Press.

Robinson, T., & Howard-Hamilton, M. (2000). The convergence of race, ethnicity, and gender: Multiple identities in counseling. Upper Saddle River, NJ: Merrill.

Rochlin, M. (1989). Heterosexual questionnaire. In Kimmel, M.S. & Messner, M.A. (Eds.), *Men's Lives* (pp. 504-505). New York: MacMillan Publishing Company.

Ruby, J. (2005). Introduction To the Special Issue on Class. *Off Our Backs,* 35(1/2), 17-18.

Sue, D. W., & Sue, D. (1999). Counseling the culturally different: Theory & practice (3rd ed.). New York: Wiley.

UN Millennium Project. (2005). *Taking action: Achieving gender equality and empowering women.* Task Force on Education and Gender Equality. London and Sterling, Virginia: Earthscan.

U.S. Census Bureau. *High School Graduation Rates Reach All-Time High; Non-Hispanic White and Black Graduates at Record Levels*. Retrieved January 20, 2006, from http://www.census.gov/Press-Release/www/releases/archives/education/001863.html

Women's Educational Media. (n.d.). *Statistics on name-calling, bullying and school violence.* Retrieved January 19, 2006 from http://www.womedia.org/lgr_statistics.htm

CHAPTER 10
CULTURALLY DISTINCT GROUPS
NATIVE AMERICANS

Culturally Distinct Groups

This information should not be used in a stereotypical fashion. Often there is a high level of heterogeneity within a group and, as educators, we should avoid the temptation, no matter how alluring, to regard culturally different groups as monolithic entities.

As professionals acquire and apply new information about different cultural groups, it is especially important to consider the varying viewpoints and values of minority group members. As previously stated, often there are within-group differences, among people from the same racial, cultural, or ethnic group. For instance, some members may have a very traditional orientation in which they endorse almost exclusively the values, viewpoints, cultural practices, customs, and language preferences of their group of origin.

In marked contrast, other members of the same racial, ethnic, or cultural group may be highly acculturated into the dominant group and have a very limited sense of identity and affiliation with their culture of origin. Instead these individuals may prefer to submerge their culture of origin in favor of the predilections expressed by the dominant culture. An example of this may be a bilingual child who has internalized a sense of shame and embarrassment about primary language. This child may refuse to speak to family members in any language but English and may prefer to associate with friends almost exclusively from the dominant culture. These attitudes are consistent with Sue and Sue's conformity stage of racial/cultural identity development. A third orientation may be one in which a person extracts elements from both the culture of origin and the new culture in which he or she finds herself or himself. This person may have a bicultural identity, meaning he or she can function equally well in both cultures. This orientation illustrates Sue and Sue's integrative awareness stage. As we examine the cultural values of each group below, it will be of critical importance to assess the degree of acculturation and assimilation before drawing any conclusions about individuals. Inappropriate application of cultural knowledge can mislead professionals into developing preconceived notions of how to work effectively with culturally distinct people.

NATIVE AMERICANS

Introduction

Do you know where the word India comes from?

_____
_____
_____

Christopher Columbus imposed the term Indian on Indians in 1492 when arrived in the Americas, mistakenly thinking he had landed in India. The term has had an enduring impact on the labeling of Indians in this country. The term Native American was later applied to Indians by the United States government in order to establish uniformity for census-keeping purposes. When applied by the government, the term includes American Indians, Alaskan natives, as well as people from U.S. territories and possessions, including locales such as American Samoa, Guam, Northern Mariana Islands, Trust Territory of the Pacific Islands, and the Virgin Islands (Haukoos & Beauvais, 1996/1997).

Let's talk about some common stereotypes we have heard. When you think about American Indians/Native Americans some common stereotypes that come to mind are?

_____
_____
_____
_____
_____
_____

https://www.youtube.com/watch?v=NCFPiFTZlHU (I'm Native, But I'm Not)

https://www.youtube.com/watch?v=xzWHxPxH08Q (Questions Native Americans Have for White People)

Discussion Question:

What surprised you when you watched these videos?

Let's look at our awareness of Native American influences in American History and Culture.

Native American Influences in U.S. History and Culture

Measure your awareness of Native American influences in U.S. history and culture.

"These days people seek knowledge, not wisdom. Knowledge is of the past; wisdom is of the future," say Vernon Cooper, spiritual elder of the Lumbee or Croatoan tribe of North Carolina. The following activity is designed to help you measure your awareness of Native American influences in U.S. history and culture and, in so doing, expand your vision of a people whose wisdom marks generations of Americans from age to age. Be sure to share this information with others.

1. Before the European Conquest, approximately how many tribes inhabited what is now the United States?

a) 50, with a population of about 500,000

b) 500, with a population of about 22 million

c) 70, with a population of about 2 million

d) 225, with a population of about 900,000

2. The present population of Native Americans in the United States is:

a) about 6 million

b) about 800,000

c) about 2 million

d) about 300,000

3. In most Native American societies, women have traditionally played a central role in:

a) the care of home and children

b) community decision-making

c) governmental and ceremonial functions of the group

d) all of the above

4. Approximately how many words were contributed to the English language by Native American cultures?

a) about 50

b) about 600

c) about 2,200

d) about 4,000

5. When they began colonizing and exploring North America, Europeans encountered many animals, plants, weather phenomena and land masses that were unfamiliar to them. Frequently the newcomers adopted and adapted Native American words to describe the environment, and many of these terms entered the English language. Below are just a few. See how many you can unscramble and discover.

1. **Animals**

   uksnk _____

   amp _____

   osoem _____

   gauraj _____

   pihckunm _____

   oocnarc _____

   sumosop _____

   ggrehci _____

   cudaarrab _____

   uoriba _____

2. **Trees and Plants**

   necap _____

   yhonamga _____

   ckihory _____

   ucacy _____

   semetuiq _____

   ccotbao _____

   minyoh _____

hsuaqs   _____

zeima   _____

ovcdaao   _____

apitoac   _____

apyaap   _____

mtotao   _____

ottpao   _____

3. **Weather Phenomena & Land Masses**

caurhiaen   _____

koohcin   _____

youba   _____

vnnasan   _____

6. Match the following Native American place names with their meanings. (Note: Four place names have the same meaning)

a. Nebraska _____

b. Massachusetts _____

c. Michigan _____

d. Ohio _____

e. Minnesota _____

f. Oregon _____

g. Kentucky _____

h. Iowa _____

i. Mississippi _____

j. North Dakota _____

k. South Dakota _____

l. Texas _____

m. Oklahoma _____

a) "good river"
b) "friend"
c) "dark and bloody ground"
d) "beautiful land"
e) "beautiful water"
f) "waters that reflect the sky"
g) "flat" or "broad river"
h) "water flowing along"
i) "I make a clearing"
j) "big river"
k) "long river"
l) "green mountain"
m) "great water"
n) "rocky hills"

7. The concept of a unified, representative government for the people was recommended to the founders of the United States by: _____

a) Canassatego, leader of the Iroquois tribe of the Northeast

b) Sitting Bull, chief of the Sioux nation

c) Powhatan, leader of the Leni Lanapi (Delaware) Nation and the father of Pocahontas

d) Tisquantum (Squanto), the English-speaking member of the Wampanoag tribe who assisted the Pilgrims in their settlement in Plymouth, Mass.

8. The founders of the United States assumed the national symbol of the bald eagle from:

_____

a) The Apache Nation

b) The Cherokee Nation

c) The Iroquois Nation

d) The Ojibwa (Chippewa) Nation

9. The victory of the Allies over the Axis Powers in World War II was due, in part, to the use of a Native American language as a secret code. Which language served as that code?

_____

a) Cherokee

b) Potawatomi

c) Sioux

d) Navajo

10. The U.S. Marine Corps Memorial Statue in Washington, D.C., honors a once-famous World War II hero of Native American descent. What is his name?_____

a) Sequoia

b) Chief Seattle

c) Senator Ben Nighthorse Campbell

d) Ira Hayes

11. True or False
a) Pocahontas is the only Native American whose portrait is painted in the rotunda of the U.S. Capitol building. _____
True or False

b) Many European colonists objected to the Native's use of water for bathing and drinking.
True or False

c) A *sachem* is a woman who represents her people as a leader in governmental or ceremonial affairs.

True or False

d) By 1993, Native Americans convinced President George Bush to sign an executive order declaring Native American tribes to be considered by the U.S. Government as sovereign "Domestic Governments" with the ability, among other state functions, to issue passports.
True or False

DEMOGRAPHICS

Demographics. In 1990, American Indians comprised .8% of the U.S. population. By the time census data were collected for the year 2000, Indian representation grew to .9%, or close to 2.5 million people. Population growth between 1990 and 2000 ranged from 26.4% to 110.3% among American Indians (U.S. Census Bureau, 2000b). This wide range is due in large part to the fact that census procedures shifted dramatically between the two collection periods. In 1990, individuals could only report a single race but by the year 2000, people could report more than one race. The upper limits of this range reflect vast increases in the people who have claimed Indian heritage. Providing self-reported information about one's American Indian heritage is very different from having a legal claim to one's Indianess.

American Indians are the only racial group in this country whose legal status has been established by the federal government. That is, in order to lay legal claim to one's Indian heritage, a person must have at least 25% blood quantum (Sue & Sue, 1999). No other racial group in this country conforms to these standards.

Discussion question:

What do you think about having to be the only group in this country that has to conform to this standard?_____

_____

_____

_____

Within the American-Indian cultural system, sharing serves an important function because it permits group members to demonstrate honor and respect for one another. In fact, refusing to share is often considered selfish and may be regarded as an offensive act directed towards the donor. Other values that have helped to sustain the American Indian include cooperation and interdependence. Within this context family needs and demands take precedence over individual needs. Group members work towards establishing and maintaining cohesion. For this reason, competition may be a very awkward construct for many American Indian children, particularly those who endorse a traditional worldview.

Current Issues

Native Americans are facing mass incarceration and policing. In states with significant Native populations they are overrepresented in the prisons. When a problem occurs on a Native reservation the unclear lines between tribal, federal and state jurisdictions make it difficult to resolve issues. Overlapping jurisdictions cause problems such as having to be tried and punished twice because you are under tribal court and federal court. Native Americans are also facing unemployment and high rates of poverty. According to the U.S. Census Bureau 27% of Native Americans live in poverty. Native Americans are still having to fight for their land. In states such as Arizona, and North and South Dakota indigenous groups are still having to fight against their land being sold or illegally possessed. Violence is another issues. Native women are 3.5 times more likely to be raped or sexually abused and over 80% of the time it is by persons NOT of the same race. Native communities are having to fight to be recognized and have their rights recognized by the federal government. Native language are on one of many considered "at risk" by UNESCO due to the fact they are dying and struggling to survive and the U.S. government is not helping. Tragically, suicide is the second most common cause of death for Native youth age 15-24 and this has yet to be addressed.

http://www.huffingtonpost.com/entry/13-native-american issues_us_55b7d801e4b0074ba5a6869c

Discussion Question:

1. What do you think are ways that we can support our Native American brothers and sisters?

_____
_____
_____
_____
_____
_____
_____

2. What have you learned that was new or that surprised you?

_____
_____
_____
_____
_____
_____
_____

Contributions to society.

Syringes, or Hypodermic Needles

Though Scotsman Alexander Wood is credited with inventing the syringe in 1853, in pre-Columbian times South American Indians used a type of syringe made from sharpened hollow bird bones attached to small bladders to inject medicine, irrigate wounds or even clean ears. Additionally, Indigenous healers also used larger and similar instruments for enemas.

Baby Bottles and Formula

Using similar technology as the syringe, the Seneca used washed, dried and oiled bear intestines with a bird quill attached as a form of nipple. Mothers filled them with a mixture of pounded nuts, meat and water.

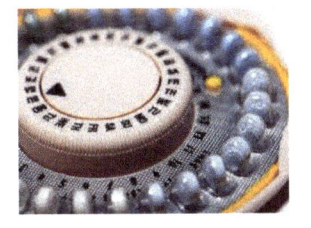

Oral Contraception

An oral contraceptive is a substance taken by mouth to prevent pregnancy. Recorded instances of American Indians taking such substances date back to the 1700s, more than 200 years before the creation of a man-made substance by western medicine. One of the herbs used was the stone seed, employed by the Shoshone, while the Potawatomi used the herb dogbane.

Cigars

On a 1,000-year-old pottery vessel found in Guatemala, a Maya man is shown smoking a roll of tobacco leaves tied with string. The Maya word for smoking was sikkar, which became the Spanish word cigarro. Once settlers had learned from Indians how to cultivate tobacco, cigar factories sprung up. One of them, an early cigar factory in Pennsylvania, gave the cigar its playful moniker the "stogie."

Pest Control

To combat insects such as lice infestation, the Paiute and Shoshone of the Great Basin, for example, washed their hair in a hot infusion made from sweetroot.

To fight other pests, pre-Columbian peoples built structures with cashew wood, while the Pima sprinkled ashes on their crops to thwart squash bugs. The Pueblo have used ground buffalo gourd to fend off garden pests, and Inca cotton farmers planted lemon verbena and burned it as a pesticide.

Petroleum Collection and Extraction

Although the discovery of oil in the United States is usually credited to Edwin L. Drake, who drilled an oil well in Pennsylvania in 1859, Native Americans were known to have sunk pits into the ground more than 400 years earlier in the Oil Creek Flats of Pennsylvania. These pits, which are 15 to 20 feet deep, were walled with vertical timbers that had been cut with stone axes.

Like many historians, J.A. Caldwell—who wrote about the oil pits—assumed the work was done by "a race of people who occupied the country prior to the advance of the Indian tribes." However, the French general Montcalm, traveling to Fort Duquesne in 1750, said he observed the Seneca and other Iroquoian Indians set fire to the oil that seeped from the ground for ceremonial fires. They also slathered protective lotion (like petroleum jelly) onto their skin.

Bunk Beds

In the Northeast of the United States, the Iroquois have long lived in longhouses—long, extended buildings made of branches formed into a large half circle and covered with bark. Inside these longhouses were bunk-beds. A creation of two beds built one on top of the other.

Pharmaceuticals

Take a step back in respect, Rite-Aid enthusiasts. According to Daniel Moerman, the foremost expert on North American Indian ethnobotany in the United States, North American Indians have medicinal uses for 2,564 plant species.

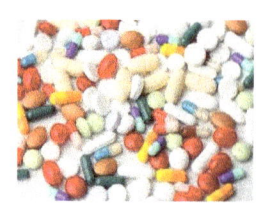

But many Native people say the actual number may likely dwarf Dr. Moerman's statistics. Since the times of the Spanish explorers, American Indian medicines have been used to cure colds with guiacum, heart ailments with dogbane, and employ foxglove and lady's slipper as a sedative. Said Steven R. King about Brazil's well-known "slobber mouth plant," the jaborandi tree, had Europeans but listened, a dry-mouth-syndrome product may have come years earlier.

Chewing Gum

Bubbulicious—remember that gum? Well it may never have gotten its start if not for the sapodilla tree. The Mesoamerican Indians chewed the milky chicle, which became today's chewing gum. And you thought you were being sneaky, Chiclets—we caught you copying Indians!

Lacrosse

This even the Europeans acknowledged at the time, but it never hurts to be reminded that Turtle Island's Indigenous Peoples created an entire sports genre. The Iroquoian Creator's game of lacrosse has been played for centuries. Yes, it was first played by the Iroquoian tribes who honored the game as one that was played for the Creator's enjoyment. We've come a long way since the Tewaaraton awards.

Follow Vincent Schilling (Akwesasne Mohawk) – ICMN's Arts and Entertainment, Pow Wows and Sports Editor . This story was originally published June 29, 2014.

Discussion Question:

What were you surprised to find out was actually an achievement by Native Americans?

_____
_____
_____
_____
_____

How does this make you appreciate and/or understand Native Americans?

_____
_____
_____
_____

In an effort to assert their self-determination, many Native Americans now refer to themselves collectively as "First Nations" people. The term "nation" implies having a systematic political structure. Native American and Alaskan native nations have very distinct democratic administrative and organizing principles.

Social and Educational Issues:

Native Americans are the only racial group in this country whose legal status has been established by the federal government. That is, in order to lay legal claim to one's Native American heritage, a person must have at least 25% blood quantum (Sue & Sue, 1999). No other racial group in this country conforms to these standards.

Christianity was closely tied to the subjugation of Native Americans. Many Christian groups sought to eradicate Native American culture by converting Native Americans to Christianity primarily through the process of education. To this end, numerous schools were erected. Eventually, boarding schools were employed as a tool to separate Native American children from their families in an effort to influence the assimilation process without parental interference. Treaties were also used to make educational provisions with Native Americans. In many schools, Native American children were forbidden to speak their indigenous tongues and when students did so, they frequently encountered corporal punishment.

NATIVE AMERICAN STUDENTS
John Watts, Assistant Director
American Indian Research Opportunities
Montana State University

One American Indian student described his reactions when he first came to Montana State University. He was in a speech communication class, and the teacher's instructions for the students' first speech were "be sure to make eye contact and project your voice loudly to be heard throughout the room." This young man became anxious. He had been taught that making eye contact or looking directly at others was combative and confrontational. He had heard elders speak in soft, even tones, and he had learned that to speak loudly is to speak boastfully. Furthermore, the other students seemed to be rewarded for rude behavior. The best students seemed to want the spotlight and relish confrontations with professors and the other students.

To be effective with American Indian students, you must be attuned to their different learning styles and cultural backgrounds. Recently a group of MSU Indian students in the American Indian Research Opportunities program participated in a discussion about their experiences at MSU. They offer several suggestions for those teaching Native American students.

"Don't stereotype us."

Indian students at Montana State University may come from one of seven different reservations in Montana, or they may be from an urban setting such as Billings. Or they could be members of an out-of-state tribe. Each tribe has its own beliefs, codes of behavior, and values. Moreover, some Indian students have been taught to follow their traditional cultures while others have adopted the values of the dominant culture. Some Indian students are well-prepared, while others face challenges adapting to the college environment. No generalization applies to all Indian students.

"I can't speak on behalf of all Indians."

Teachers sometimes place unwarranted stress on Indian students in classes where the content relates to American Indians. They call on the Indian students to give the Native American perspective. This demand can make the students feel uncomfortable because they know that there is a wide variety of viewpoints among Native Americans; no individual can be an expert on every aspect of Indian culture. You should not assume that all Indian students are well acquainted with their own heritage. However, Indian students can be valuable resources. An appropriate strategy is to speak with them before hand to see if they have knowledge on a topic and if they feel comfortable speaking about it.

"We're not angry about the past; we are upset about today's racism."

Indian students, especially those from reservations, have boldly stepped into the very different world of the university, but they are sensitive to racism whether it is intentional or unintentional.

"We are family-oriented."

Strong connections to extended family, a strength back home, may impose hardships on students attending school. They may be expected to go home for funerals even for relatives who you may consider distant. Indian students who come from reservations are far from their homes, families, and support systems. They may feel that they are living in an alien culture, which may contribute to their being lonely and depressed.

"If we're quiet, that doesn't mean we are not paying attention."

This conduct may arise from a variety of sources including the desire not to show themselves as being better than other Indian students or not to appear to act "white."

Many Indian students prefer to blend in rather than stand out.

"Our thought processes may be different."

Studies of American Indian cognition (cited in Wright 59) indicate that there "may be important differences in perceptions of the world, of time, of the emotional content of nonverbal vocalizations, and of the meaning of teachers' behavior between American Indians and Anglos."

"English may not be our first language."

A few students may speak English as a second language, so they may be reticent about speaking up in class or may need to use tutoring services such as the Writing Center.

"We don't want special treatment; we just want a fair chance."

You should make yourself available to assist American Indian students who need help, but you should not assume that because a student is Indian, his or her academic preparation is weak. The following suggestions are culled from research into teaching American Indians and other minorities. Many of these strategies also apply to non-Indian students. In fact, non-Indian rural students share some of the culture shock that Indian students may experience when they arrive at SDSU. Also, they may not apply to every Indian student. So the best advice is to remain flexible and use a variety of teaching strategies and learning activities.

- Practice personal warmth plus high expectations
- Respect cultural differences.
- Learn the cultural resources of your students.
- Develop multiple instructional approaches.
- Be aware of the ways you ask questions.

- Remember some students do not like to be "spotlighted" in front of a group.

- Be aware of proximity preferences - how close is comfortable?

References

Haukoos, G., & Beauvais, A. (1996/97, Winter). Creating positive cultural images: Thoughts for teaching about American Indians. Childhood Education, 73(2), 77-82.

Sue, D. W., & Sue, D. (1999). Counseling the culturally different: Theory & practice (3rd ed.). New York: Wiley.

CHAPTER 11
CULTURALLY DISTINCT GROUPS
AFRICAN AMERICANS

African American's have a very unique experience and position within American society. From the remnants of slavery to the fight for equality during the civil rights movement; African Americans have often been in underprivileged and discriminatory positions. The fact that this has also been influenced by race and certain distinctive characteristics has resulted in many negative perceptions as well as the creation of a negative self-image. Throughout this workshop we will discuss topics that relate to problems that many African Americans' encounter and how it can affect both their educational and life experiences. These topics include:

- Poverty
- Discrimination/Prejudice
- Culturally Incompetent Instruction
- Peer Relations

As a beginning activity take time to analyze how possible stereotypes and biases are formed. These questions are all about giving initial honest perceptions and there are no right or wrong answers.

First Thoughts

Look at each of the words below and write down the first two or three adjectives which come to mind (your thoughts or traditional ideas). Positive or negative, just write down your first thoughts.

Disabled: _____

New Yorkers: _____

Californians: _____

Teachers: _____

Elderly: _____

Women: _____

Jews: _____

Whites: _____

American Indians: _____

Gays: _____

African American: _____

Men: _____

Police Officers: _____

Irishmen: _____

Managers: _____

Resident Advisors: _____

A Students: _____

Now let's build on this initial exercise and examine some thoughts and perceptions about African Americans.

1 When you think about African Americans some common stereotypes are?

2. What are some positive perceptions that you attribute to African Americans?

3. What are some negative perceptions about African American people or their communities?

Poverty

While poverty isn't something solely related to African American people and their communities, it is often associated with minorities in general because they're likelier to come from a lower socioeconomic status when compared to the majority of white people.

Of the 45 million African Americans in the United States, 28.1% fall beneath the poverty line. This is an alarming statistic compared to the 11.8% of all Americans who fall under the poverty line ("2013 Black Population"). These impoverished African Americans tend to all have similar characteristics, despite their location. They are more likely to be raised by a single parent, with government assistance, in a cash based economy with high unemployment and a focus on unskilled labor in addition to heavy influences of drugs and crime (Lewis, 1966; Noguera, 2003).

The poverty that poor African Americans experience is often different from the poverty of poor whites. It's more isolating and concentrated. It extends out the door of a family's home and occupies the entire neighborhood around it, touching the streets, the schools, the grocery stores.

A poor black family, in short, is much more likely than a poor white one to live in a neighborhood where many other families are poor, too, creating what sociologists call the "double burden" of poverty. The difference is stark in most major metropolitan areas, according to recent data analyzed by Rutgers University's Paul Jargowsky in a new report for the Century Foundation.

In five-year American Community Survey data from 2009-2013, more than a third of all poor African Americans in metropolitan Chicago live in high-poverty census tracts (where the poverty rate is above 40 percent). That number has gotten worse since 2000. And it's about 10 times higher than for poor whites (Badger, 2015).

Racial disparities in concentrated poverty

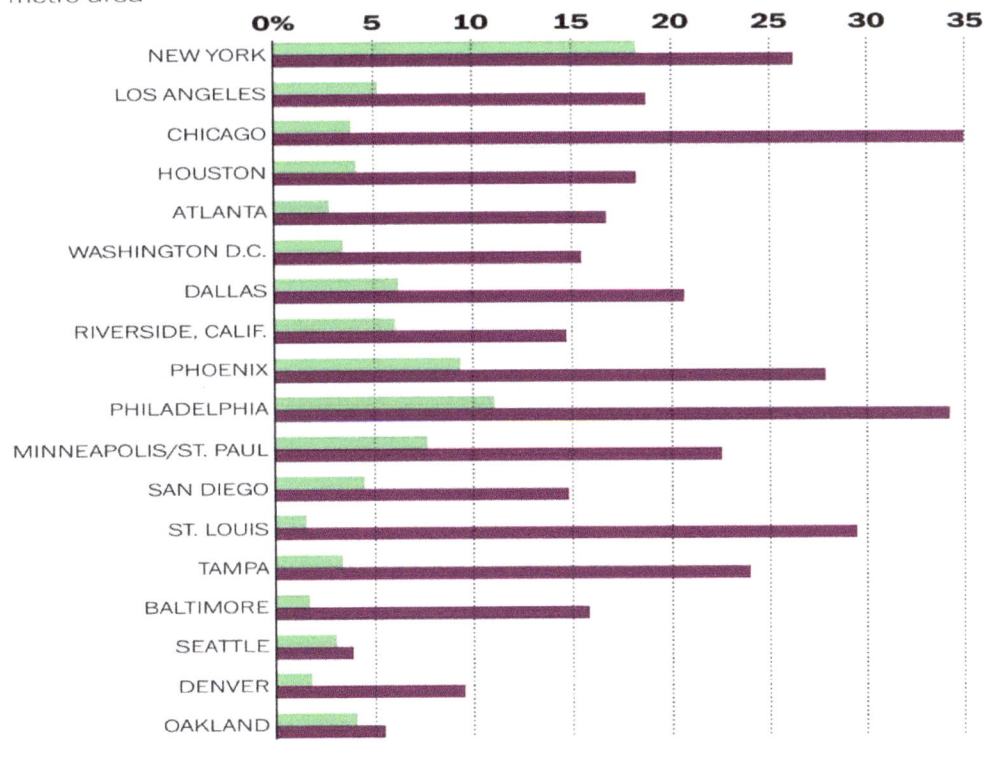

Percentage of poor **blacks** and **whites** living in concentrated poverty, by metro area

Metro area	
NEW YORK	
LOS ANGELES	
CHICAGO	
HOUSTON	
ATLANTA	
WASHINGTON D.C.	
DALLAS	
RIVERSIDE, CALIF.	
PHOENIX	
PHILADELPHIA	
MINNEAPOLIS/ST. PAUL	
SAN DIEGO	
ST. LOUIS	
TAMPA	
BALTIMORE	
SEATTLE	
DENVER	
OAKLAND	

WAPO.ST/**WONKBLOG**
Source: The Century Foundation analysis of 2009-2013 American Community Survey data

This definition of "double poverty" is something that many African American's experience. The concentration of poverty in particular neighborhoods normalizes and reinforces detrimental environmental factors within these impoverished places. The fact that many of these places are simply regarded as urban neighborhoods further exacerbates the problem. It is hard for one to fully realize the effects of poverty if it is assumed that it is a common and normal position for people in a specific demographic. In many ways this shapes many African American's outlook as they feel that living in an impoverished environment is what is expected of them within

America's society. As a result, people within this demographic may view themselves as inferior and begin to doubt that they can be successful.

Discrimination/Prejudice

In discussing discrimination and prejudice it is important to understand that in many ways this has been a constant for African American people since the inception of the United States. Slavery is often looked at as the most blatant example of discrimination, but even though slavery has been abolished for over 150 years discrimination towards African Americans has remained. It is important to also remember that not all discrimination is direct and that it also can be presented at an institutional level. This can be represented within the workforce but also the educational system as well.

For instance, black pre-schoolers are far more likely to be suspended than white children, NPR reported. Black children make up 18 percent of the pre-school population, but represent almost half of all out-of-school suspensions.

Once you get to K-12, black children are three times more likely to be suspended than white children. Black students make up almost 40 percent of all school expulsions, and more than two thirds of students referred to police from schools are either black or Hispanic, says the Department of Education.

Even disabled black children suffer from institutional racism. About a fifth of disabled children are black – yet they account for 44 and 42 percent of disabled students put in mechanical restraints or placed in seclusion.

When juveniles hit the court system, it discriminates against blacks as well. Black children are 18 times more likely to be sentenced as adults than white children, and make up nearly 60 percent of children in prisons, according to the APA. Black juvenile offenders are much more likely to be viewed as adults in juvenile detention proceedings than their white counterparts (Institutional Racism, 2015).

These disparities are also present within the workplace with black college graduates twice as likely as whites to struggle to find jobs - the jobless rate for blacks has been double that of whites for decades. A study even found that people with "black-sounding names" had to send out 50 percent more job applications than people with "white-sounding names" just to get a call back.

And it gets progressively worse as the pay scale gets higher. For every $10,000 increase in pay, African American's percentages of holding that job falls by 7 percent compared to whites (Institutional Racism, 2015).

While the discrimination within the work force alone is discouraging, it is also further complicated by the intense criminalization of African American people in general. In using the term criminalization, it is meant to represent the fact that intent is often assumed without finding proper causation or reason beforehand. For African American's experiencing this type of discrimination it can cause of high levels of stress and neuroticism.

A black man is three times more likely to be searched at a traffic stop, and six times more likely to go jail than a white person. Blacks make up nearly 40 percent of arrests for violent crimes.

Blacks aren't pulled over (and subsequently jailed) more frequently because they're more prone to criminal behavior. They're pulled over much more frequently because there is an "implicit racial association of black Americans with dangerous or aggressive behavior," the Sentencing Project found (Institutional Racism, 2015).

Discrimination towards African Americans is still very prevalent within our society. It is important that this discrimination is acknowledged but also discouraged. Societal constructions should be conducive to the attainment of success rather than responsive to potential failures

AFRICAN AMERICANS

During the 1993-1994 school years, African American youngsters accounted for 15.5% of public school enrollment although only 6.8% of teachers were African American (National Center for Education Statistics, 1995). Arguably, the percentage of African American teachers should reflect the proportion of African American students in the population. Such ratios provide a host of benefits. As an example, minority teachers frequently understand and can respond effectively to the cultural experiences that children of color bring to school. Additionally, minority teachers often serve as role models, and their presence communicates in subtle and indirect ways that minority children are capable of achieving academically. Further, children who are members of the dominant culture begin to accept the fact that people of color can assume positions of leadership. Nationwide, African American youngsters accounted for 16.9% of the student population, 8.5% of students receiving gifted education services, 20.6% of the special education population, and 33.4% of all suspensions (Education Trust, 1998). Currently, professional and scholarly references to people of African origin generally use the term "African American." There is no consensus, however, among some African Americans about this label. While some people regard the term African American as more accurate, others prefer the term "Black" because it has social and political connotations. Still others believe that the term "African American" does not adequately reflect their West Indian or South American roots. Immigrants throughout the African Diaspora, such as those from Jamaica, the Bahamas and continental Africa may assign more salience to their specific country of origin. Throughout this document we use the term "African American" because it provides a more accurate and encompassing label to describe African-origin people in the United States. When interacting with

African Americans, we recommend that people ask individuals about their personal preferences in this regard.

Economic despair, poverty, poor health, crime, violence, and inadequate education are among the challenges that impact the African American social experience in this country (Campbell-Whatley, Obiakor, & Algozzine, 1997). Often educational difficulties are construed as pathological. Historically, attempts to understand African American children and their families were couched in pejorative terms that enlisted almost exclusively, deficit viewpoints of intellectual functioning and family life. Less attention, however, has been devoted to the strengths of African American children and their families. Cultural values.

Educators motivated towards ethical practice and cultural competence recognize he cultural context of student learners from diverse backgrounds (Day-Vines, 2000). They also recognize that these cultural contexts may differ markedly from their own.

Many of the cultural values prevalent in African American communities have their origins in West Africa (Holloway, 1990). As is the case with many non-Western peoples, some dominant American cultural values and African American values are often at odds. For instance, an American cultural orientation or worldview promotes individualism, competition, material accumulation, religion as distinct from other parts of culture, and mastery over nature. In marked contrast, many African Americans, particularly those with very traditional worldviews, embrace values such as the significance of the collective versus the individual, kinship and affiliation, spirituality, connectedness, harmony with nature, and holistic thinking (Akbar, 1985; Asante & Gudykunst, 1989; Myers, 1987; Nobles, 1991).

Black Racial Identity Development Model

Pre-encounter

The African American has absorbed many of the beliefs and values of the dominant White culture, including the notion that "White is right" and "Black is wrong." Though the internalization of negative Black Stereotypes may be outside of his or her conscious awareness, the individual seeks to assimilate and be accepted by Whites, and actively or passively distances him/herself from other Blacks.

Encounter

This phase is typically precipitated by an event or series of events that forces the individual to acknowledge the impact of racism in one's life. For example, instances of social rejection by White friends or colleagues (or reading new personally relevant information about racism) may lead the individual to the conclusion that many Whites will not view him or her as an equal. Faced with the reality that he or she cannot truly be White, the individual is forced to focus on his or her identity as a member of a group targeted by racism.

Immersion/Emersion

This stage is characterized by the simultaneous desire to surround oneself with visible symbols of one's racial identity and an active avoidance of symbols of Whiteness. As Thomas Parham describes, "At this stage, everything of value in life must be Black or relevant to Blackness. This stage is also characterized by a tendency to denigrate white people, simultaneously glorifying Black people..." (1989, p. 190). As individuals enter the Immersion stage, they actively seek out opportunities to explore aspects of their own history and culture with the support of peers from their own racial background. Typically,

White-focused anger dissipates during this phase because so much of the person's energy is directed toward his or her own group and self exploration. The result of this exploration is an emerging security in a newly defined and affirmed sense of self.

Internalization

While still maintaining his or her connections with Black peers, the internalized individual is willing to establish meaningful relationships with Whites who acknowledge and are respectful of his or her self-definition. The individual is also ready to build coalitions with members of other oppressed groups.

Internalization-Commitment

Those at the fifth stage have found ways to translate their "personal sense of Blackness into a plan of action or a general sense of commitment" to the concerns of Blacks as a group, which is sustained over time (Cross, 1991). Whether at the fourth of fifth stage, the process of Internalization allows the individual, anchored in a positive sense of racial identity, both to perceive and transcend race proactively.

Black Racial Identity Attitudes and Stages of the Life Span: An Exploratory Investigation

A major contribution to the understanding of the African American personality has been the nigrescence models a.k.a. racial identity development theory "Nigrescence" is defined as the "developmental process by which a person becomes Black, where Black is defined as a psychological connection with one's race rather than pertaining to their skin color" 1970's: models constructed to analyze the psychological profiles of Black Americans in response to the civil rights movement

Cross's Nigrescence Model: 1971 4 themes of racial identity:

Theme 1: Pre-encounter: Pre-discovery of one's racial identity

- Attitudes are pro-white and anti-black
- Thinks in terms of White frame of reference (devalues/denies Blackness)
- Does not realize implications of being a Black American

Theme 2: Encounter: Significant racial incident causes the individual to explore their Black identit

- individual makes a conscience decision to develop a Black identity

Theme 3: Immersion-emersion: following the encounter experience, the individual immerses himself in Black culture

- Wears ethnic clothing
- Black hairstyles,
- Associates only with Blacks, etc.)

Theme 4: Internalization: Individuals become comfortable with racial identity

- Wants to be acknowledged for being Black
- More aware of what being Black means
- Recognizes and appreciates other ethnic heritages

Culturally Incompetent Instruction

In working with all minority populations it is important to make sure that educators are using culturally competent teaching methods. This has become even more important as these populations have begun to dominate much of the student body within the public school system. Especially in regards to subjects like history, it is important that instructors are cognizant that most U.S. History textbooks are written from a specific White-American perspective. It is important to educate from a multicultural perspective that is fully inclusive of the student body. For African Americans, it is important that they learn more about their history beyond slavery and Martin Luther King Jr. It is also important that multiculturalism is preached in place of assimilation so that all student feel properly engaged and represented within their school. Commonalities are never a bad thing, but they shouldn't be overvalued to the point that cultural awareness and knowledge are afterthoughts.

Something also disheartening is the practice of remediating problems so that the learner conforms to school expectations, rather than structuring school tasks in ways that respond to the students' strengths. With the current emphasis on the inclusion of all learners in classrooms, it seems essential to change that practice.

Another achievement problem is the serious inequity that results when certain cultures value behaviors that are undervalued in school.

Research about the African-American culture shows that students often value oral experiences, physical activity, and loyalty in interpersonal relationships (Shade 1989, Hilliard 1989). These traits call for classroom activities that include approaches like discussion, active projects, and collaborative work. In contrast, many mainstream white Americans value independence, analytic thinking, objectivity, and accuracy. These values translate into learning experiences that focus on competition, information, tests and grades, and linear logic. These patterns are prevalent in most American schools (The Culture/Learning Style, 1994).

While children may not be able to identify specific reasons why they often can recognize the feelings of inclusion/exclusion. Naturally, when someone feels that they're excluded the motivation to succeed within the realm begins to wane. I think that by valuing more collaborative work and being cognizant of African American culture, many students from that demographic would become more engaged and successful.

Peer Relations

Positive peer relations are essential to all humans' development. Yet, in minority groups it isn't preached or valued particularly within education. In addition to poverty, many African American children develop and become accustomed to living within dysfunctional environments. This can be represented within the home or the community as a whole. If they aren't getting the opportunity to learn positive social skills from their social environment it makes the school environment that much more impactful. However, many schools don't educate students on how to positively interact with their peers or directly discourage bad and offensive behavior. Positive peer interaction can also be a beneficial factor in motivating students and children to do well in their respective activities. For African American students this can prove even more essential in making them feel like they belong in the particular setting that they're in. While education may not be valued within the home, a positive social climate will further encourage them to want to continue attending school and doing well. It can be extremely detrimental to one's well-being if both they're home environment and social environments are distressing.

Conflict is something that will naturally occur within life. However, for many African American students they're at a disadvantage because they haven't been directly educated on positive methods for conflict resolution. Often the educational system can use negative punishment instead of positive reinforcement. Disciplinary actions like suspensions and expulsion can be warranted, but if students are never fully encouraged and supported to do well then they may never realize the benefits of positive social interactions.

References

Akbar, N. (1985). Community of self. Tallahassee, FL: Mind Productions.

Asante, M. K., & Gudykunst, W. (Eds.). (1989). Handbook of international and intercultural communication. Newbury Park, CA: Sage.

Campbell-Whatley, G. D., Obiakor, F., & Algozzine, B. (1997). Effects of innovative programming on youngsters at-risk. Journal of At-Risk Issues, 4(1), 3-9.

Cross, W. E. (1991). Shades of Black: Diversity in African American identity. Philadelphia: Temple University Press.

Holloway, J. E. (1990). *Africanisms in American culture*. Bloomington: Indiana University Press.

Day-Vines, Norma L. (2000). Ethics, Power, and Privilege: Salient Issues in the Development of Multicultural Competencies for Teachers Serving African American Children with Disabilities.

Digest of Education Statistics, 1995. (1995, October 23). Retrieved July 31, 2017, from http://nces.ed.gov/pubsearch/pubsinfo.asp?pubid=95029

Education watch: the 1998 Education Trust state and national data book, vol. II. (1998). Washington, D.C.: Education Trust.

McIntosh, P. (1989, July/August). White privilege: Unpacking the invisible knapsack. Peace and Freedom, 10-12.

Myers, J. (1987). Balance without bias. Currents, 13(4), 34-42.

Nobles, W. (1991). African philosophy: Foundations for Black psychology. In R. Jones (Ed.), Black psychology (3rd ed., pp. 47-53). Berkeley, CA: Cobb & Henry.

CHAPTER 12
CULTURALLY DISTINCT GROUPS
EUROPEAN AMERICANS

White Racial Identity Models:

Racial/ethnic identity development is conceptualized as a series of stages through which individuals pass as their attitudes towards their own racial/ethnic group and the White populations develop, ultimately achieving a "healthy identity."

4 stages: generally speaking….. 1. Acceptance of the stereotypes the dominant society has attributed to the group. 2. Conflict or dissonance individual begins to question the previously held stereotypes. 3. Immersion in the culture of the racial/ethnic group and rejection of individual's ad values outside the group. 4. Positive racial/ethnic identity retained while coming to accept the positive attributes of individuals and cultures outside their reference group.

Concerns with WRID models:

- Before the WRID models were introduced, it was assumed that an individual's racial/ethnic identity evolves in response to an oppressive dominant society.
- Helm describes Nigrescence as consisting of "stage of racial identity that may evolve in response to the common experience of resisting racial discrimination."

Helm's White Identity Development Model: 5 stages

1. contact – accept status quo and lack awareness of their selves as racial beings

2. disintegration – experience conflict

3. reintegration – Pro-white and anti-Black

4. pseudo-independence – intellectual acceptance of blacks

5. autonomy – achievement of positive White racial identity

   a) Attitudes that most Whites develop about their own group and other racial/ethnic groups reinforced by stereotypes of dominant society the system of oppression impacts the racial attitudes of both Whites and racial/ethnic minorities but is experienced differently.

   b) The purpose of the WRID models is to "explain how Whites develop(ed) attitudes toward their racial group membership" but they end up merely describing how Whites develop different levels of sensitivity to and appreciation of other racial/ethnic groups, but little about White identity.

   c) The Helm model states that some people fixate at some stage prior to autonomy or may even skip stages because of particular environmental circumstances.

It is claimed that White racial identity issues focus on Blacks as the primary outgroup "because White racism in the US seems to have developed as a means of justifying the enslavement of Black Americans."

The Conceptualization of White Racial Consciousness

- White racial consciousness is defined as "one's awareness of being White and what that implies in relation to those who do not share White group membership."
- Although individuals develop racial attitudes and these attitudes often change over time, there is no evidence that the process of changing attitudes is developmental; therefore, racial attitudes may vary with situational influences.
- Racial attitudes change following, and as a result of experiences that cause dissonance in the person's cognitive structures or schemas.

White Racial Consciousness Statuses:

Unachieved white racial consciousness: lacking exploration, commitment, or both.

1. *Avoidant type:* lack of consideration of one's own white identity as well as avoidance of concern for racial/ethnic minority issues.

2. *Dependent type*: commitment to some set of attitudes regarding white racial consciousness, but no personal consideration for alternative perspectives.
    - this situation may be the result of excessive dependence

1. *Dissonant type* : clearly uncertain about their sense of white racial consciousness and racial/ethnic minority issues
    - their uncertainty causes them to be open to new information, but they lack commitment to the ideas they might express

Achieved white racial consciousness: achievement of some kind of integrated personal outlook on racial attitudes 4 types:

1. *Dominative type* : characterized by a strong ethnocentric perspective, which justifies the dominance of racial/ethnic minority peoples by the majority culture view the White

Americans and the majority culture in the US as superior and of more value than minorities and their associated cultures. White culture is considered to be superior because they have achieved more due to their intelligence and personal attributes, and therefore, are entitled to the advantages they receive. However, a minority in the same position is the result of cunning evil and blind luck.

2. *Conflictive type* : those that are opposed to obvious, clearly discriminatory practices, yet are usually opposed to any program or procedure that has been designed to reduce or eliminate discrimination. They believe that racial/ethnic minorities experience = opportunities and advantages and their lack of achievement is the result of factors such as deviant value or lack of motivation

3. *Reactive type :* those aware of racial/ethnic discrimination as a significant feature in American society and react to this acknowledgement. They believe that White Americans benefit from and are responsible for the existence of discriminatory attitudes and practices.

4. *Integrative type* : persons that are comfortable with their whiteness as well as comfortable interacting with visible racial/ethnic minority people

Moving Between Statuses and Types:

There is no evidence to support the belief that racial attitudes follow a developmental sequence movement between the statuses and types of White racial consciousness is not seen as necessarily sequential or predictable, but as a variable consequence of life experiences social conditions may create what appears to be a developmental process, where people move from one type to another, but different social conditions can also create a reverse movemen

CHAPTER 13
CULTURALLY DISTINCT GROUPS
MIDDLE EASTERN

CHALDEAN STUDENTS

Many people recognize the name Chaldean as an ethnic group in the Bible (Jer 50:10; Ezek 11:24) or as a distinct rite of the Catholic church. To residents of Chicago, southern California, and especially Michigan, Chaldeans are a commonly recognized ethnic group. When informally surveyed, however, even Michigan residents were largely uninformed about their Chaldean neighbors. With over 100,000 ethnic Chaldeans residing in southeast Michigan (Sengstock, 2005) and increasing immigration due to the Iraq war, college professionals who understand the Chaldean community may be poised to increase recruitment, retention, and better serve Chaldean students on their campuses.

Some general information about Chaldeans

First, Chaldeans, in spite of their Iraqi origin, generally consider themselves ethnically Assyrian or Chaldean, distinct from their Arab neighbors. Their native language, Soureth, is of Semitic origin and the modern-day derivation of Aramaic, the language spoken by Jesus of Nazareth. Aramaic remains the liturgical language of the Chaldean church, much as Latin was the liturgical language of the Roman church until 1963. Many American-born Chaldeans may speak Soureth, Arabic, or both, in addition to English. According to Sengstock (2005), only 23 Chaldeans resided in Michigan in 1923; by 1986 there were 10,000, and in 2005, there were approximately 100,000. Petrosian (2006) noted that one third of all Christians in Iraq left the country in the 1990s. The Christian population in Iraq further plummeted between 700,000 and 900,000 in 2003 to about 360,000 in 2006 (Library of Congress, 2006).

To define Chaldean and mainstream-American identities, we focus on four contrasting values: *collectivism, uncertainty avoidance, religion, and masculinity.*

A limited number of researchers have investigated Chaldean- Americans. Some investigators have focused on Chaldean- American history (Sengstock, 2005, 1982) and patterns of immigration (Sengstock, 2005, 1982; Rubin and Bhavnagri, 2001; Shikwana, 1997). Others have studied Chaldean- American values in relation to collectivism (Sengstock, 1982, 2005;Shikwana, 1997; Rubin and Bhavnagri, 2001), uncertainty avoidance (Goffe, 1999; Sengstock, 1982; Shikwana, 1997), religion (Sengstock, 1982, 2005), and masculinity or gender roles (Gallagher, 1999; Sengstock, 1982). Doctoroff (1978) studied the perceived identities of first-generation Chaldean high school students, and Sengstock (1982, 2005) investigated how Chaldean-Americans viewed their identity in relation to given variables. Education-related studies have been limited to primary and secondary levels, concentrating especially on the attitudes and perceptions of education in the community (Sengstock, 1982; Shikwana 1997), and relations between educators and students (Evans-Bruns, 1984; Rubin, 2001). Until now, no study has focused on the identity or values of second-generation Chaldean- American college students.

In a study conducted by Michigan state and using a protocol from a similar study on Japanese undergraduates (Brender, 2006), the researchers compiled and adapted a list of interview questions for Chaldean-American college students. The researchers recorded a pilot study with a volunteer participant and then modified, added, and eliminated questions based on the responses.

The investigators sent personalized emails to students with Chaldean surnames, soliciting undergraduates who identified as American-born Chaldeans between the ages of 18 and 24, and whose parents identified as Iraqi-born Chaldeans. The researchers also recruited participants through campus flyers, a university web-based announcement, and word of mouth. Ultimately a convenience sample of 13 students was obtained.

Participants provided demographic information regarding age, major, parental origins, and Most institution related questions were designed to solicit perceived differences between Chaldean and mainstream American values. Questions about hobbies and activities were also asked as a way to better understand personal values. Finally, to shed further light on personal identities, participants were asked to draw and then explain a picture that would depict their cultural identity.

Researchers compiled field notes then analyzed each category, looking for commonalities and differences between Chaldean and mainstream-American values.

Representative quotes were selected, analyzed, discussed, and ultimately edited for conciseness. The researchers interviewed 13 second-generation Chaldean- American college students from one urban university in the Midwest. Five men and eight women participated, between ages 19 and 22. Six were sophomores, four juniors, two seniors, and one did not specify. Most students belonged to pre-medical programs. Fourteen of the participants' parents were from Baghdad and eight were from the village of Telkaiff, often considered the cradle of Chaldean civilization. The researchers found that participants associated Chaldean identity with collectivism. uncertainty avoidance, religious fervency, and disparity in gender roles. Conversely, participants associated mainstream American identity with individualism, a willingness to embrace new experiences, limited regard for religion, and gender equality. Findings are addressed for each of the above values:

Participants overwhelmingly regarded collectivism as a principal value in the Chaldean community, in contrast with the individualism they generally associated with mainstream

Americans. Collectivism in this study was defined as: "Attending to and fitting in with others and the importance of harmonious interdependence with them" (Markus and Kitayama, 1991, p. 224). As such, participants associated collectivist values with strong family and community ties and an overriding concern with family reputation.

The importance of family was a dominant theme in each interview. Students frequently discussed their bonds with immediate and extended family. When asked what constituted success in life, male and female participants mentioned family before career or personal happiness. One participant answered:

> *Being a good father. I think this is important--being able to raise your kids and [having] other people . . . say, "Wow, look how good these kids are!*

Another participant expressed that Chaldean family-ties were probably stronger than those of non-Chaldean families:

> *My mom definitely devoted every minute . . . to my dad and her kids. Considering that I was a babysitter, this clearly wasn't the case with [non-Chaldean] families . . . Like, [Chaldean parents] don't have their own little adult time to go . . . to a movie and leave the kids at home.*

Family collectivism in the Chaldean community was often enhanced by a family-owned business, most notably a party or convenience store. One participant insisted, "When you work with your family at an early age you also become more tight-knit with them." Finally, many participants discussed the importance of maintaining face, which included preserving personal and family reputations within the Chaldean community. As one participant explained:

Uncertainty Avoidance

Hofstede (1984) defined uncertainty avoidance as "the extent to which members of a culture feel threatened by uncertain or unknown situations" (p. 113). In this study, Chaldean-American college students described members of the Chaldean community as high in uncertainty avoidance, which they associated with close family proximity, tightly controlled dating norms, and a value for education only as it related to financial security. Uncertainty avoidance was evidenced in the tendency for parents and their college-age children to remain in close proximity. Students frequently discussed their own and others' decisions to commute rather than live on college campuses. Iraqi-born parents were often described as discouraging if not forbidding their college-age sons or daughters from leaving home. The following statement was representative:

> *[Chaldean parents] don't want anybody outside of the house yet and . . . that's certainly been the case with a lot of my friends. They've chosen between [two local universities] just because they're [close to] home.*

Though theoretically not opposed to marrying outside the Chaldean community, most participants revealed a preference for a Chaldean marriage partner. Some articulated that marrying within the Chaldean community offered a greater likelihood of sharing similar values. Such values, including a prohibition of divorce, seemed to offer as much certainty as one could reasonably hope for.

In terms of education, participants insisted that many Chaldean Americans prized medicine, pharmacy, law, and business for their prestige, but mostly for their imminent road to financial security. Studying or dabbling in the arts, humanities, and social sciences was general invalidated. Learning for the sake of learning, according to one female participant, is not highly valued in the Chaldean community.

Although a few participants spoke to their family's premium on education, most revealed that their parents' vision of schooling equated to security. A biology major whose parents held advanced degrees, expressed the importance of education in terms of uncertainty avoidance:

I've always been brought up with, like, education is something that is very important because you don't know when you could just lose everything.

When asked what kind of man her parents would like her to marry, one student said: [It's important that] he has money. Doesn't matter if he went to school or anything like that--as long as he's successful.

Religion was a dominant theme in each interview. As descendants of Christian minorities in a predominantly Muslim country, participants frequently discussed religion in terms of identity and how it set them apart from both Arab Muslims and American Christians. Participants overwhelmingly viewed their religion, whether Roman or Chaldean Catholic, as key to their identity, lifestyle, and personal spirituality.

While participants generally saw themselves and other Chaldean Americans as more religiously fervent than other Americans, many also felt a need to distinguish themselves from Muslims from their homeland and other parts of the Middle East. A female participant insisted:

When you say you're Arab, it's just like they're Muslim--they practice different things, they eat

In terms of lifestyle, many participants discussed their involvement with the church and church organizations. A 19 year-old participant described how his faith set the framework for participation in various religious activities:

I am still volunteering at [a Catholic church]. And I do CLC--Chaldeans Loving Christ-- which is a youth group . . . For me, I don't see how religion can't play a major role in people's lives. [If I didn't have religion], I would have no idea where I'd be right now

Some participants claimed that their participation in Catholic rituals went beyond the custom for most Roman Catholics. During the Lenten season--the 40-day period where Catholics make individual sacrifices—one participant reported:

> *For . . . Lent--I give up all animal products. I even do Sundays . . . Just because I feel like you're not making sacrifices if you don't include Sundays.*

Beyond identifying as Catholic and following prescribed rituals and traditions, participants often discussed deeper aspects of their spirituality. Without prompting, students frequently talked about faith. Typical of these comments was the following:

> *Whenever I'm lost or I don't know what to do, I turn to God. I tell Him whatever is bothering me or whatever I need. If I need help or whatever . . . He always comes through.*

Religion was a prevailing theme in each interview. When asked to draw a picture to represent personal identity, many respondents featured crosses, bibles, or churches to represent their Chaldean identity or a universal Christian identity that shined above all other identities.

Masculinity

Hofstede (1984) defined masculinity as competitiveness, which included disparity in gender roles. Although competition may be a feature among Chaldeans, especially regarding business ownership, many participants focused on gender-role differences regarding career choice, roles within the family, and double standards in dating.

Gender Roles: Career Choice

Many male and female participants discussed boundaries for women planning a career. Perceptions ranged from parents forbidding their daughters to work to parents encouraging their daughters to study medicine. At one extreme, a participant revealed:

My father was always like, "In my household, as long as I am living here and paying the bills, a woman will never work!"

In other families, Iraqi-born parents were seen as encouraging women to pursue careers, but not careers that might interfere with family responsibilities:

My two older brothers . . . were in medical school and [my sister] wanted to be a doctor but my dad said to her, "You should become a pharmacist because it's better for you--you're gonna raise a family."

Gender Roles: Family

Students frequently described gender-role differences between their fathers and mothers. One informant claimed her father was representative of other Chaldean fathers:

My dad was your typical, "You're-not-going anywhere!"-- very powerful at my house; where my mom didn't really have a say in a lot of things. But then again, she didn't care to have a say.

Mothers were often portrayed as homemakers and nurturers. One student related:

Chaldean women take care of family. They're not used to having any responsibility other than the house. They were raised ever since they were girl . . . [to] just take care of the kids, and teach them how to behave, and prepare them food and take care of the house.

Many women explained that their parents defined success for women based on marriage and family. When asked how her parents would envision an ideal life for her, one female participant replied, "Married, popping children, and helping [my husband] out at the party store."

Double Standards in Dating

Although male and female participants agreed that men and women should abstain from premarital sex and date only with intentions of marriage, several also admitted that repercussions for dating applied only to women. While many felt their parents would never allow their daughters to date, most conceded that their parents would or had encouraged their sons to date freely. Although punishment for a disobedient daughter was beyond the frame of reference for some respondents, one male participant imagined his reaction to a sexually active daughter:

> *A guy screwing around is not a big deal--that's just the way it is. But it's not okay. I wouldn't say it's okay . . . , but I wouldn't be so mad if I found out my son screwed around. But . . . if my daughter did that, I would tell her to leave the house!*

Female participants, in contrast, typically identified double standards in dating as an injustice, although most claimed to capitulate to their parents' wishes. One woman commented:

> *My extended family, they would always ask my brother, "So, do you have a girlfriend yet?" He's 18 now and done with his first year of college. If I said I had a boyfriend, . . . they'd stake me on the outside!*

References

Brender J. Handbook of evaluation methods for health informatics. Burlington, MA: Elsevier Academic Press; 2006.

Bruns, C. E. (1984). *Teaching English as a second language and culture to Chaldean-American immigrants in occupations related to the food and beverage industry.*

Goffe, L. (1999). Chaldean's USA. The Middle East, 50.

Hofstede, G. (1984). *Cultural dimensions in management and planning.* Asia Pacific journal of management, 1(2), 81-99.

Library of Congress Law Library: An Illustrated Guide, 2005, *. (2006). Place of publication not identified: Publisher not identified.

Markus, H. R., & Kitayama, S. (1991). Culture and the self: Implications for cognition, emotion, and motivation. Psychological review, 98(2), 224-253.

Petrosian, V. (2006). Assyrians in Iraq. *Iran and the Caucasus, 10*(1), 113-148. doi:10.1163/157338406777979322

Sengstock, M. C. (2005). *Chaldeans in Michigan.* East Lansing, MI: Michigan State University.

Sengstock, M. C. (1982). *Chaldean-Americans: changing conceptions of ethnic identity.* New York: Center for Migration Studies.

Shikwana, T. (1997). *The relationship of socioeconomic status of Chaldean parents and their childrens education.*

Rubin, L., & Bhavnagri, N. P. (2001). Voices of Recent Chaldean Adolescent Immigrants. *Childhood Education, 77*(5), 308-312. doi:10.1080/00094056.2001.10521655

CHAPTER 14
CULTURALLY DISTINCT GROUPS ASIAN AMERICANS

ASIAN AMERICAN STUDENTS

A Collection of Cultures Within a Group

Asian cultural groups living within the United States are usually seen as a homogenous population group. There are many preconceived ideas surrounding these groups and as is true with stereotypes they are often incorrect. Asia is a continent, so referring to someone as simply "Asian" overlooks major parts of their culture and identity.

There are 48 countries that make up Asia, differing in language, religion, and culture. This part of the world has around 4.4 billion people living in it, and according to the U.S. census in the United States about 6% of the population)17 million people identify as Asian or Asian-American.

Some questions before starting

-What places usually come to mind when you think of an Asian person?

-What do you know about Asian culture(s)?

-What do you think when others refer to Asian people as "Chinese"?

Demographics within the U.S.

According to the U.S. Census:

There are 17 million people who identify as Asian or Asian-American in the United States, which translates to 5.6% of the total population.

Some states with the highest number of Asian people are: California, New York, Texas, and New Jersey. States with the highest percentage of Asian populations are: Hawaii (57.4%), California (14.9 %), New Jersey and Nevada (9% each).

New Jersey and Nevada

It may come as no surprise that California and Hawaii place high in the ranks of total population as

According to the American Immigration Council, New Jersey has had a significant increase in Indian immigrants, and most of the immigration has been related to the business sector. This has significantly boosted the economy in specific counties.

Nevada has also seen a considerable increase in its Asian population, according to the website American Progress this has been mostly through working permits and family visas the population is rapidly growing.

Terminology

Asian-American

It is very important to keep in mind that Asian-American is a term that encompasses an extremely diverse number of people. Asian people alone are more than half of the world's total population. It is frequently overlooked that places such as Russia and middle-eastern countries are actually part of the Asian continent, but in the U.S. not all of them fall under the "Asian" categorization.

The definition of what makes one "Asian-American" in the US census is described as: A person having origins in any of the original peoples of the Far East, Southeast Asia, or the Indian subcontinent including, for example, Cambodia, China, India, Japan, Korea, Malaysia, Pakistan, the Philippine Islands, Thailand, and Vietnam."

Oriental

The term "oriental" is ***not*** a correct way to refer to a person who is Asian-American. According to NPR the term has a history of racism and stereotypical imagery. In fact, the term is incorrect enough to have been outlawed from government usage in New York.

This term is one also created with erroneous ideas of a "flat world" being that the orient is a relative term regarding one's placement in the world. The term Oriental also perpetuates the idea of Asian-Americans as foreigners that belong elsewhere.

Asian Pacific Islander (A.P.I.)

As mentioned previously the term "Asian" has been problematic throughout history because of the incredibly large number of people included by its classification. According to the PEW research center, up until 1990 Pacific Islanders were grouped under the Asian classification. API populations felt their experiences differ greatly from the other groups included in the Asian classification and there will be further distinctions made in the 2020 census.

Video: What kind of Asian are you?

https://www.youtube.com/watch?v=DWynJkN5HbQ

Stereotypes

What are some common stereotypes you might think of when you think of people who are Asian?

Are any of them positive stereotypes?

How about negative?

Common Stereotypes

Asian=Chinese

A common stereotype in the U.S. is that Asian and Chinese is the same thing. Although it may seem obvious to point out, people in the Asian-American population can be from many different cultures. An Asian-American person can be just as American as anyone else, but if they are immigrants it does not mean they all come from China. China is just one of the countries in Asia, and just because Chinese-Americans are the largest Asian-American population (23% according to the PEW research center), it doesn't mean it is correct to assume a person who is Asian-American is Chinese. Chinese-Americans were some of the first people to come from Asia as labor workers, at one point there was such a hostile attitude towards them that immigration from China was banned. With this information in mind, it's easier to understand how this stereotype is still alive today.

All Asians are smart

When people think about an Asian person there is the running offensive joke that "all Asians are good at math" or that "all Asians are super smart." Despite it being true that the Asian-American communities often place high value on education, and according to asia society.org 49% of this population is college educated; this stereotype places an unfair amount of pressure on Asian-Americans to perform to unrealistic expectations.

The Model Minority Myth

According to NPR, The Model Minority Myth is the idea that Asian-American groups are able to overcome the hardships of minority status in the U.S. by hard work and family values. Poon, Squire, Kodama, Byrd, Chan, Manzano, Furr & Bishundat (2016) describe this myth as follows: "This racial stereotype generally defines AAPIs, especially Asian Americans, as a monolithically hardworking racial group whose high achievement undercuts claims of systemic racism made by other racially minority populations, especially African Americans." This stereotype is not one singular idea but many that come together to form this myth, from the assumption of high achievement in work and school to better financial status, many of the stereotypes surrounding Asian-Americans come from this myth. Poon et al., (2016) highlight the importance of one of the driving forces behind this myth, which is that the Asian-American Model Minority fabrication was used to further perpetrate racism against African-Americans (as well as other minorities) by inaccurately comparing their experiences. Poon et al., (2016) also note that it is important to consider the higher status immigration offers some Asian-Americans were given for coming into this country, and how the lower status Asian-American populations are removed from the Model Minority narrative.

The Asian-American experience is the same for all Asians.

As noted earlier, Asian-Americans are a group that is made up by many cultural groups. What one group might experience is very different from what another might go through. For example, the experience of a Japanese-American raised by college educated parents with middle class status is largely different from one of a Vietnamese-American raised by parents who came to this country as refugees and might not speak the language or have qualifications for higher paying jobs. A group as diverse as Asian-Americans can mean different experiences between subgroups and within them as well.

Video: Asian-Americans respond to stereotypes

https://www.youtube.com/watch?v=hPioJP39dW4

Asian-Americans are a group that is extremely diverse, and as it can be seen today with the distinction made between APIs and Filipinos in 2020, will probably gain more clarification between subgroups instead of a monolithic image. It is important to remember this moving forward, to be able to break stereotypical thinking and create culturally sensitive interactions with this growing population.

Asian Americans are often thought of as high academic achievers. However, an overlooked and growing population of Asian American students are at risk educationally and may need additional programs and services to help them succeed in college.

Asian American College Students Who are Educationally at Risk

While Asian Americans and Pacific Islanders (AAPIs) are growing faster than any other racial group in the U.S., they are all but invisible in higher education, and generally ignored in the research literature, and thus greatly misrepresented and misunderstood. The concept of educational risk is generally not associated with Asian American students. Indeed, the tremendous growth in the number of Asian American students attending colleges and universities over the past decade obscures the fact that members of some Asian American ethnic groups have prospered in higher education while others have struggled to enter and remain in the educational system (Bennett and Debarros, 1998).

For example, while 58.4 percent of Indian and Pakistani Americans have completed college, only 2.9 percent of Hmong Americans have college degrees (Ng, 1995). Numerous misinterpretations of similar data have led to the stereotyping of Asian Americans as a group of high-achieving students who possess the skills and knowledge needed to succeed at all levels of their education (Alva, 1993; Chun, 1995; Dao, 1991; Hu, 1989; Nakanishi, 1995; Siu, 1996; Suzuki, 1977, 1989). Unfortunately, for many Asian American students who are having academic difficulty, this perception of guaranteed educational success has proved detrimental because their needs have been systematically neglected at the institutional level. Most studies on educationally at-risk students have focused on African American and Latino students or students at the elementary and secondary school level (Dao, 1991; Dolly, Blaine, and Power, 1989; Johnson, 1994; Presseisen, 1988; Rossi, 1994; Slavin, Karweit, and Madden, 1989). The retention of Asian American at-risk students at the postsecondary level is not regarded as an issue of concern, presumably due to the belief that post-secondary education goes is considered the basic level of education needed in the United States.

Asian American Students and Acculturation Asian American students who have lived most, if not all of their lives, in the U.S. may have mixed feelings about acculturation into American society (Kim & Omizo, 2005). Acculturation is defined as adapting to the normative process of the dominant culture (Kim & Omizo).

Some examples of acculturation are: assuming English as one's primary language, adapting to Western societal values, and displaying mannerisms normative in American society (Lee, Choe, Kim, & Ngo, 2000). An individual's acculturation of Western culture can vary depending on the length of time lived in the U.S., regional location, socioeconomic status, and demographics of the community (McCarron & Inkelas, 2006).

Many first-generation students in higher education acculturate to Western culture much faster than their immigrant parents (Lee et al.). It is common for family members who immigrate to America to reject acculturation by consistently using their native language, practicing traditional lifestyles and cultural norms, and by forcing their children to abide by their native cultural values (Lee et al.). Asian American students are typically perceived as having either traditional or Western values.

Asian Americans who hold traditional values are characterized as valuing interdependence, harmony, collectivism, and hierarchy in family structure (Chang, 1996; Kim & Omizo, 2005). In contrast, Western culture is perceived to value individualism, autonomy, future-oriented thinking, and competition (Kim & Omizo). Both Western and traditional Asian values guide how Asian American students think, feel, and behave throughout their college experience (Kim & Omizo). Traditional Asian values can be enforced by parents, family, and community, but are often rejected by students who believe it is beneficial to follow Western culture (Lee et al., 2000). Studies have shown that some Asian American students who adopt these opposing sets of values may lead to conflict when attending college while living at home (Aldwin & Greenberger, 1987). Also, possessing both Western and traditional Asian values can result in a pessimistic personality, or feeling guilty, anxious, or both (Zane, Sue, Hu, & Kwon, 1991). Kim and Omizo (2005) stated that Asian American students can find resolution by integrating Western and Asian cultures into their daily interactions on campus. Student integration is defined as becoming proficient in the dominant culture while simultaneously maintaining their set of indigenous cultural values. Psychologically, integration for Asian American students, as well as many other racial identities, can allow cultural values to be expressed in both Western and Asian American systems, particularly when cultural values are in opposition.

Many Asian Americans have settled and integrated into Western culture, giving an outward perception of "content conformity." This conformity may reinforce the assumption that Asian Americans do not need the support and resources afforded to other diverse groups.

Asian American students with immigrant parents have frequent intergenerational arguments concerning language usage and cultural relations. Lee et al. (2000) stated, "family acculturation conflicts are more likely to occur among recent immigrants where the gap between parents and children is greatest" . Because of the differences between the rate of acculturation with U.S.

born Asian Americans and immigrant parents, known as the "acculturation gap," consistent conflicts and miscommunication can take place at home. Family conflict and miscommunication can also be due to parents' lack of knowledge about U.S. higher education. "Evidence suggests that first-generation students encounter a lower perceived level of family support, a lower level of importance placed on college by parents, and less knowledge of the college environment and campus values among parents" (McCarron & Inkelas, 2006,). For example, parents may lack knowledge of available financial resources, institutional terminology and language, academic support, and the role of a college advisor, mentor, or both (McCarron & Inkelas). Parents' lack of knowledge of higher education can lead Asian American students to experience "culture shock" (Inman & Mayes, 1999). This can lead to negative outcomes for the student, such as depression resulting from environmental discomforts, the misinterpretation of financial awards and assistance, and eventual withdrawal from classes (McCarron & Inkelas).

One of the leading causes of mental health struggles among Asian American students is the pressure to adhere to the traditional values that prevent them from expressing their social and psychological difficulties (Cress & Ikeda, 2003). In particular, many first-generation college students and individuals who identify closely with Asian values feel embarrassed to go to counseling because having any psychological problems is believed to bring shame and humiliation to their family and community (Kim & Omizo, 2005; Atkinson et al., 1990).

Asian Americans who primarily embrace Asian traditional values seek social accord, which leads them to hide their emotional expression and internalize their depression (Cress & Ikeda). Within higher education, there are some resources in place for Asian and Asian American students to further explore their own racial identity. Yeh and Wang (2000) suggested that student affairs professionals should implement support programs for Asian American students, such as research initiatives, student mentoring, and Asian American clubs.

Asian American college students coming from Asian immigrant families have a high instance of depression or mental health concerns on campus due to several causes: acculturation to Western culture, pressure from parents to succeed, and pressure to embrace the model minority myth. For example, Asian American first-year students struggle with transitions due to pressures to acculturate to college campus norms. Student affairs professionals can help with transition and support for Asian American students on campus by being cognizant of the developmental hardships associated with the process of acculturation. Student affairs professionals should provide outlets for social interactions with others who hold the same traditional values.

Campuses can also support Asian American parents by setting up programs specifically catering to understanding the resources in higher education. Student affairs professionals also need to ask themselves if acculturation to Western values is helpful or hindering to Asian American students. Being acculturated can lead to more comfort when utilizing services like campus-based counseling and an overall easier transition into college life, but it can also conflict with cultural values and traditional practices, such as discrepancies within the family and community relations. Asian American students are continually changing their cultural values to fit into college climate. It is time for our higher education system to expand and deepen their knowledge of Asian culture to best serve the Asian American student population. Student affairs can begin to accommodate these students by supporting social groups and clubs that cater to Asian American culture. Not only do these clubs provide a service to the university, they also create a safe space for students to cope with their mental health concerns and provide a social community. As the Asian American student population grows in higher education, so does the demand for social support.

REFERENCES

Aldwin, C., & Greenberger, E. (1987). Cultural differences in the predictors of depression. American Journal of Community Psychology, 15, 789-813.

Atkinson, D., Whiteley, S., & Gim, R. H. (1990). Asian American acculturation and preferences for help providers. Journal of College Student Development, 31(2), 155-161.

Chang, E. C. (1996). Cultural difference in optimism, pessimism, and coping: Predictors of subsequent adjustment in Asian American and Caucasian American college students. Journal of Counseling Psychology, 43(1), 113-123.

Cheng, L., & Espiritu, Y. (1989). Korean businesses in Black and Hispanic neighborhoods: A study of intergroup relations. Sociological Perspectives, 32, 521- 534.

Cress, C. M., & Ikeda, E. K. (2003). Distress under duress: The relationship between campus climate and depression in Asian college students. NASPA Journal, 40(2), 74-97.

Inman, E. W., & Mayes, L. D. (1999). The importance of being first: Unique characteristics of first-generation community college students. Community College Review, 26, 3-22.

Kim, B. S. K., & Omizo, M. M. (2005). Asian and European American cultural values, collective self-esteem, acculturative stress, cognitive flexibility, and general self-efficacy among Asian American college students. Journal of Counseling Psychology, 52(3), 412-419.

Lee, R. M., Choe, J., Kim, G., & Ngo, V. (2000). Construction of the Asian American family conflicts scale. Journal of Counseling Psychology, 2, 211-222.

Liao, H., Rounds, J. K., & Andreas, G. (2005). A test of Cramer's (1999) helpseeking model and acculturation effects with Asian and Asian American college students. Journal of Counseling

Psychology, 3, 400-411.

Mallinchrodt, B., Shigeoka, S., & Suzuki, L.A. (2005). Asian and Pacific Island American students' acculturation and etiology beliefs about typical counseling presenting problems. Cultural Diversity and Ethnic Minority Psychology, 3, 227-238.

McCarron, G. P., & Inkelas, K. K. (2006). The gap between educational aspirations and attainment for first-generation college students and the role of parental involvement. Journal of College Student Development, 47(5), 534-549.

Okagaki, L., & Frensch, P. A. (1998). Parenting and children's school achievement: A multiethnic perspective. American Educational Research Journal, 35(1), 123-144. Solberg, V. S., Ritsma, S., Davis, B. J., Tata, S. P., & Jolly, A. (1994). Asian American students' severity of problems and willingness to seek help from university counseling centers: Role of previous counseling experience, gender, and ethnicity. Journal of Counseling Psychology, 41(3), 275-279.

Yeh, C., & Wang, Y. (2000). Asian American coping attitudes, sources, and practices: Implications for indigenous counseling strategies. Journal of College Student Development, 41(1), 94-103.

Yoo, H. C., & Lee R. M. (2005). Ethnic identity and approach-type coping as moderators of the racial discrimination/well-being relation in Asian Americans. Journal of Counseling and Psychology, 52(4), 497-506.

Zane, N. W. S., Sue, S., Hu, L., & Kwon, J. (1991). Asian American assertion: A social learning analysis of cultural differences. Journal of Counseling Psychology, 38, 63-70.

CHAPTER 15
CULTURALLY DISTINCT GOUPS LATINO AMERICANS

Latinx

A uniformed group, but not really.

We live in a country that is made up of diverse cultural groups. Often we classify those groups without knowing much about them. We might know a bit about what a certain group looks like or certain stereotypes, but it can be hard to be truly knowledgeable about many groups outside of our own. Latinos are a group that is regularly seen as "one" singular culture in this country, and although Latin-American countries do share some similarities in culture, there are many variations within the group itself. From language to location or religion, Latino and Latin-American populations can be very different from one another.

A few questions before starting:

1) Who would you say is Hispanic? How about Latino?

_____
_____
_____
_____

2) Are Mexican-Americans Hispanics?

_____
_____
_____
_____

3) What does Chicano mean to you? Have you heard this term before?

_____
_____
_____

4) What do Latinx and Chicanx mean?

_____

_____

_____

_____

5) Do Latinos speak Spanish?, Explain your response

_____

_____

_____

_____

Demographics within the U.S.

According to the Census:

56.6 million Americans fall under the classification of "Hispanic/Latino" (which is 17.6% of the total U.S. population). The Latino population is projected to be 119 million by 2060.

According to the PEW research center:

The largest population growth happened within Latinos/Hispanics from 2000-2014. Some areas such as North Dakota, Pennsylvania, and Georgia are seeing anywhere from a 91% to a 365% increase in their Latino/Hispanic populations.

The states with the highest number of Latino people are California (15 million), Texas (10.4 million), and Florida (4.8 million). An interesting note to make is that despite California having the highest number of Latinos/Hispanics the state with the highest percentage of Latinos/Hispanics is New Mexico, with 48% of its population falling under this demographic.

Terminology

Although the terms Hispanic and Latino are used interchangeably that does not mean it is accurate or even correct to do so.

Hispanic

According to Gratton & Merchant (2016), after decades of debate of whether or not to create a new identifier that would separate Mexican, Puerto Rican, Cuban, Central and South American, or "other Spanish" from other races was included in the U.S. census. This new term became "Hispanic."

However, the term Hispanic is based on language. It means "of Spanish speaking origin." Spanish speaking origin can mean many different things in this country, it could mean anything from a Dominican immigrant, or a third generation Mexican-American who might not even speak Spanish, or an undocumented migrant from El Salvador. It is easier to notice then, how a term encompassing such a diverse group of people does not fit everyone.

Latino

According to NPR being Latino is defined as "any person of Latin American descent residing in the United States," how that compares to Latin-Americans is that those people who fall under "Latin-American" are people living in those countries at this time and not in the USA. This is where there is often confusion; Latin-America can include countries that are *not* Hispanic. Brazil is a Latin-American country in which Portuguese is spoken, therefore not falling in the Hispanic categorization. Other examples include the Dutch-speaking Suriname, French Guyana, or Haiti.

Latinx

Latinx is a newer term, and according to Robyn Henderson-Espinoza(PhD) is designed to include people who would fall under the "Latino" category but it is an inclusive term for queer, trans, men, women, and gender non-conformists.

Chicano/Chicanx

The term Chicano has a complicated history and can have different meanings depending on the period in time or the person that it is being used for.

According to the Hispanic American, the term Chicano derived from the derogatory term "chicamo" used to refer to recently arrived Mexican immigrants by Texans in the early 20th century, mainly Mexican-Americans. It is also said to have ties to the indigenous Nahuatl language in which "x" sounds are often pronounced as "ch" sounds, making "Mexicanos" now "Mechicanos." As time passed, activists in the 1960s made an effort to reclaim this term as a source of pride in heritage and indigenous identity.

As suggested by Simmen & Bauerle (1969) a chicano during their time could be seen as "An American of Mexican descent who attempts through peaceful means to correct the image of the Mexican-American and improve the position of this minority in the American social structure." It is not hard to understand then, that this term often comes with political undertones. Today this term is used by Mexican-Americans to describe their own identity between the American and Mexican cultural identities. It should be noted that other Latinx people should not be called Chicanx as it applies only to Mexican-American people, and even in those cases it is best to address it with the person who might or might not identify as such.

Latin-American

As previously mentioned NPR defines Latin-American as: "the people that currently live in Latin-America." Latin-America includes about 30 countries depending on the technicality of the definition. Those countries are all in Central and South America. A large percentage of these countries were colonized by Spain which has led to similarities in language and culture, that does not mean however that the culture in these countries is monolithic

Is it Latinx, Hispanic, Chicanx or something else?

After learning the previous information, it should become easier to know which terms are better suited for different people and populations. That doesn't mean that everyone agrees on these terms.

The issues with the term Hispanic

Although some people might fall under the Spanish speaking category, it should be kept in mind that it does not automatically make them Hispanic. By definition this might the case, but not everyone wants to use this term. Countries that speak Spanish today have ties to Spanish colonization in history. For those countries it meant that their indigenous populations were enslaved, killed, and forcibly converted onto the dominant religion. Having fought for and gained independence from Spain allowed for those countries to form their own separate cultural identities; for some the term Hispanic is one that still ties them to a country and culture that they are not part of and do not wish to be a part of.

Another problem with this term is that it is mistakenly used for certain Latinx people. Brazilian people are often mistaken for Hispanic, when their language is Portuguese since the country was colonized by Portugal. The same is true for countries like Suriname or Haiti, in which Spanish is not spoken despite being part of the Latin-American Countries.

A person from Spain could very well be Hispanic, therefore complicating the term even further by grouping together the Colonizer with its former colonies.

Issues with Latinx/Latino

Latino or Latinx are very broad terms. People who are considered Latinx may not agree with the label because it erases part of their culture. If one becomes Latino they are no longer Cuban, Mexican, Chilean, therefore some would rather be Cuban-American, Mexican-American and such denominations. An important survey in 2015 from the PEW research center showed that most Latinx/Hispanics believe that their heritage is their race, meaning that they see Mexican, Honduran, or Costa Rican as their race.

Issues with Chicanx

As mentioned previously, the term Chicanx comes with political history. Some people have differing ideas of what this term means. For some people it may mean strictly someone that is associated with the Cesar Chavez farmer movement of the 60s. For others it might be associated with an idea of the term being offensive. There are also people who take pride in reclaiming the term and enjoy having a separate term to define the "in between" feeling that comes with being neither full Mexican nor American. Although in present time the term is used to describe people who are Mexican-American, it is best not to refer to someone as Chicanx unless that person doesn't have a problem with it or prefers it.

Issues with all of the previous terms

It is important to remember that the terms Latinx/Latino, Hispanic, Chicanx/Chicano are terms that were used by the U.S. to classify groups of people. People from in Latin-American countries don't think of themselves in these terms. They are simply Argentinos, Cubanos, Mexicanos and so on. It should also be remembered that although a person can fit into a certain category for a term, that does not mean that term is adequate to be used on that person. It is always best to have the person themselves let others know on what term is preferred.

Video about Hispanic/Latino terms

https://www.youtube.com/watch?v=gs2tdjzla8Y

Stereotypes

Latinx=Mexican

Often when people think of Latinx/Hispanic people in the U.S. the first thing that comes to mind is "Mexican.' It is very important to remember that there are many countries that are included in the Latinx demographic, in fact, according to Encyclopedia Britannica there are at least 30 countries that make up Latin-America (depending on the definition of "Latinx" accepted). Just as a Japanese person is not the same as a Thai person, a Brazilian person is not a Mexican person simply because they are both Latinx.

Latinx=Undocumented

Although it is true that undocumented immigrants are more likely to be from Central and South America, the Migration Policy Institute estimates that there around 11 million total undocumented immigrants coming from many different regions of the world, such as Africa or Asia and even Canada. There are tens of millions of Latinx people in the United States that are not undocumented, news media and politics regularly focus on only the undocumented populations making them seem much larger than they really are.

Latinx= Brown

If one is to think of a "Latino" the image that is more likely to come to mind is that of a person of brown skin that is Mexican, and other Latinos are expected to be some variation of that idea. A Latinx person can have features that can largely vary from person to person, even within a specific country of origin. From white skin and "European" features, to African features and dark skin Latinx populations don't have a "set" look. The mixing of different races has given way for people to have features that can be found in different places of the world outside of Latinx countries, as well as indigenous features from a variety of groups. Even Mexico has a population of often forgotten Afro-Mexicanos.

Latinx people speak Spanish.

This has already been discussed, but it is still a very common stereotype. As mentioned previously even within Latin-American countries not everyone speaks Spanish, and when considering Latinx in the U.S. there is great variety. Some people might have heritage from a Hispanic nation and still not speak the language. Spanish is a shared language among most Latin-American countries, but it is not the default language for Latinx people, since they are living here in the U.S.

Video on Latinx diversity

https://www.youtube.com/watch?v=vLwiacjdGEo

Conclusion

There is no "right" answer to choose from when referring to a specific person since they are the ones that can inform you on the correct term they prefer. However there are terms that are often misused and can end up not only incorrect but also being offensive. A person can consider themselves Latinx, Hispanic, Chicanx, Latin-American or something else entirely. With that in mind, the information presented today it can make it easier to distinguish between the populations and the terms that are commonly used to classify them. The Latinx population is regularly stereotyped, but now that the more common stereotypes have been discussed it should be easier to interact with these populations with a greater sense of clarity.

Family Oriented

An individual is strongly identified with and attached to his family.

Family refers to both the nuclear family and the extended family.

There are strong feelings of loyalty and reciprocity among members of the family.

Familly closeness may serve to protect individuals against stress by providing a support system (Triandis, Marin, Betancourt, Linsansky & Chang, 1982).

Bien/Mal Educado

Related to the importance of the family is the importance of being *bien educado*.

A direct translation of this term is "well-educated".

However, in Spanish *bien educado* refers to being brought up well, that is, that an individual's parents brought the individual up to be a well-behaved, respectful a person with values

Collectivism

Related to the importance of family is the belief in collectivism. Hispanics tend to view the needs of the group as superceding the needs of the individual.

This means that sometimes the individual has to sacrifice something for the good of the group Marin & Triandis, 1985

Simpatía

This word appears to mean sympathy but has a different meaning in Spanish. It better translates to pleasantness and congeniality.

Simpatía refers to behaviors and actions that promote pleasant relationships.

These behaviors include behaving respectfully and in ways which promote harmony and avoid conflict (Marin and Marin, 1991).

Respeto

Respeto is related to simpatía. Personal power is derived from being treated respectfully in interpersonal relations. Therefore, a person who is considered to be powerful is treated very respectfully **(Marin & Marin, 1991)**.

Importance of Education

There is a stereotype that Hispanics don't value education. In fact, Hispanic families do greatly value education. In a recent poll, 95% of the Hispanic parents surveyed responded that they believed a college education was very important (Brown, 2005). What may differ, however, is how they show that they value education.

Traditionally in Hispanic culture, the teacher is viewed with great respect. The teacher and the school are seen as the experts in education. Because of the high respect with which the teacher is held, parents will be reluctant to question the teacher, to give suggestions, or to appear to be interfering in the educational process. This may give the appearance of not valuing education. In addition, socioeconomic status can affect how a parent interacts with the school. Parents with low SES may be working several jobs which do not allow the parent to attend school meetings These factors combine to make it appear that the parents do not value education (Brown, 2005).

However A lack of homework help and low attendance at school meetings, should not be perceived as not valuing education. In general, Hispanics do believe that an education is important for their children.

Language.

Some Hispanics are bilingual. Other Hispanics are monolingual Spanish-speaking or monolingual English-speaking. In other cases, a Hispanic family may speak an indigenous language as a first language, Spanish as the second language and English as a third language

Personal Space

Personal space refers to the amount of physical space that is considered culturally appropriate between people (Hall, 1969).Hispanics have been found to prefer a smaller personal space. That is, they feel more comfortable when physically close to others (Marin & Marin, 1991).

Time Orientation

There is a difference between future and present-oriented cultures. Future-oriented cultures emphasize planning for the future and value punctuality.

Present-oriented cultures tend to place more emphasis on what is occurring at the present moment. There is a more flexible view of time. Hispanics tend to be more present oriented. The quality of the interpersonal interaction is more important than the length of time (Hall, 1969; Hall, 1983; Marin, 1987, Hall, 1969; Hall, 1983; Marin, 1987,Marin & Marin, 1991).

If you want to hold a meeting with Hispanic parents. You may need to have translators, if you are not proficient in Spanish (language use). You will need to allow for time to establish respect for your audience as well as show an interest in them and their lives (respeto and simpatía). There may not be as many questions as you anticipate. Cultural communication is an ongoing process. Mistakes are inevitable, but sensitivity to cultural and communication issues can enhance the quality of education for all students. Unfamiliarity with cultural communication differences can lead to misinterpretation, misunderstanding and even unintentional insult Cultures are continually evolving

References

Banks, J. (2003). *Multicultural education: Issues and perspectives, 4th edition.* New York: John Wiley & Sons.

Bernstein L.L. (2005) *Communicating Across Cultures in Schools.* PP Georgia Department of Education

Brislin, R. (2000). *Understanding culture's influence on behavior, 2nd edition.* New York: Harcourt School Publishers.

Brown, S. (2004, Fall). Confronting myths about Hispanics. *Community Connections: Local Education Funds, 11*(1).

Hall, E. T. (1969). *The hidden dimension.* Garden City, NY: Doubleday Anchor Books.

Hall, E. T. (1983). *The dance of life: The other dimension of time.* Garden City, NY: Anchor Press/Doubleday.

Jacobson, M.F. (1998). *Whiteness of a different color: European immigrants and the alchemy of race.* Cambridge, MA: Harvard University Press.

Kroeber, A. L., & Kluckhohn, C. (1963). *Culture: A critical review of concepts and definitions.* New York: Vintage Books.

Ovando, C. J., Collier, V. P., & Combs, M. C. (2003). *Bilingual and ESL classrooms: Teaching in multicultural contexts, 3rd edition.* New York: McGraw Hill.

Marín, G. & Marín, B. V. O. (1991). Research with Hispanic populations. *Applied Social Research Methods Series, Vol. 23.* London: Sage Publications

CHAPTER 16
LGBTQ+

LGBTQ +

The LGBTQ+ community is a cultural group that has similarities to others, but is also completely different. Previously, groups referring to ethnicity, race and culture have been the topic—but anyone can be LGBTQ+. Whether they are Latinx, Asian-American, white, Native American etc., this cultural group can be even more diverse than the ones discussed in past workshops. LGBTQ+ people face high rates of discrimination and hate crimes as well. According to a publication by the Social Justice Advocacy center by the University of Central Florida, LGBTQ+ is an acronym for people (Lesbian, Gay, Transgender, Queer and others) that are brought together by having gender identities or sexual orientations that differ from the heterosexual and cisgender majority.

A few questions before starting:

-How would you define Gender? Is that different from sex?

_____
_____
_____
_____

-Have you heard that being LGBTQ+ is a choice? If so how do you feel about that?

_____
_____
_____

-Which terms do you find most confusing and why?

_____
_____
_____
_____

Demographics within the U.S.

Getting accurate and detailed demographics for this population is not as simple as it might be for others. For example, it can be much easier to give out a survey in which someone selects the race/ethnicity that applies to them, as opposed to one in which they disclose their sexual orientation or gender identity (which might come with negative connotations in society). The Williams Institute of UCLA estimates that about 9 million (3.5%) people in the U.S. identify as part of the LGBT community.

This same report notes that:

-Younger people tend to report being LGBTQ+ at higher rates than their older counterparts

- LGBTQ+ populations do not differ in race or ethnicity in significant ways when compared to non-LGBTQ+ populations.

- Adults are more likely to identify as LGB/T in the Northeast and West than in the South and Midwest.

-Although there is existing national information about LGBTQ+ populations, most of the questions in surveys have addressed only LGB/T terminology and they have lacked questions about gender identity.

Terminology

There are many terms under the LGBTQ+ umbrella, hence the "+" after the acronym. It is important to recognize that the terms for gender identity can be fluid or static for some, and are constantly changing. These terms can mean different things for different people, as the resource center for LBTQIA+ in UC Davis puts it: The explanations of the terms given that follow should be taken as a starting point for discussion and understanding.

According to the LGBTQIA+ Resource Center glossary from UC Davis (Quoted segments are directly from the glossary):

Gender

"A social construct used to classify a person as a man, woman, or some other identity. Fundamentally different from the sex one is assigned at birth."

It is important to recognize that the idea of gender is a social construct, meaning that it is something that can change and has changed throughout time and societies. The social norms and roles that define "male" or "female" are constantly changing and are not the same in every society. It also must be recognized that Gender *does not* equal the sex assigned at birth, "biological sex" does not define gender.

Cisgender

"A gender identity, or performance in a gender role, that society deems to match the person's assigned sex at birth. The prefix cis- means "on this side of" or "not across." A term used to call attention to the privilege of people who are not transgender."

-Being Cisgender does not mean someone is a "good" or "bad" person because of it. Being privileged from it means that the way society is structured favors cisgender people.

Lesbian

"A woman whose primary sexual and affectional orientation is toward people of the same gender."

Gay

"A sexual and affectional orientation toward people of the same gender; can be used as an umbrella term for men and women."

Bisexual

"A person whose primary sexual and affectional orientation is toward people of the same and other genders, or towards people regardless of their gender."

-Bisexual can mean different things for different people, but most commonly it is used to describe people who are attracted to their opposite and same gender.

Queer

"One definition of queer is abnormal or strange. Historically, queer has been used as an epithet/slur against people whose gender, gender expression and/or sexuality do not conform to dominant expectations. Some people have reclaimed the word queer and self identity as such. For some, this reclamation is a celebration of not fitting into norms/being "abnormal." Manifestations of oppression within gay and lesbian movements such as racism, sizeism, ableism, cissexism/transphobia as well as assimilation politics, resulted in many folks being marginalized, thus, for some, queer is a radical and anti-assimilationist stance that captures multiple aspects of identities."

-Queer is a special term in that (as mentioned previously in the above definition) it is a term that has been reclaimed from its previous offensive connotations, and included as a way to embrace being "different" from what "normal" should be.

Intersex

"People who naturally (that is, without any medical intervention) develop primary or secondary sex characteristics that do not fit neatly into society's definitions of male or female. Many visibly Intersex people are mutilated in infancy and early childhood by doctors to make the individual's sex characteristics conform to society's idea of what normal bodies should look like. Intersex people are relatively common, although the society's denial of their existence has allowed very little room for intersex issues to be discussed publicly. *Hermaphrodite* is an outdated and inaccurate term that has been used to describe intersex people in the past."

-The term *hermaphrodite* should not be used. Despite this term still being found in certain textbooks and other sources it is still an outdated and inaccurate term. It should be noted that surgeries during infancy to assign a certain biological sex are more often than not a mistake rather than a "correction."

Asexual

"A sexual orientation generally characterized by not feeling sexual attraction or a desire for partnered sexuality. Asexuality is distinct from celibacy, which is the deliberate abstention from sexual activity. Some asexual people do have sex. There are many diverse ways of being asexual."

Pronouns

" Linguistic tools used to refer to someone in the third person. Examples are they/them/theirs, she/her/hers, he/him/his. In English and some other languages, pronouns have been tied to gender and are a common site of misgendering (attributing a gender to someone that is incorrect.)"

-Pronouns are important to address when interacting with LGBTQ+ individuals. It is not up to the person using the pronouns to decide which are appropriate for the person they are referring to, instead the person who is being referred to should get to decide their preferred pronouns. It can be as simple as introducing one's own preferred pronouns and then addressing the other's preference.

Coming Out

"'Coming out' describes voluntarily making public one's sexual orientation and/or gender identity. It has also been broadened to include other pieces of potentially stigmatized personal information. Terms also used that correlate with this action are: "Being out" which means not concealing one's sexual orientation or gender identity, and "Outing, " a term used for making public the sexual orientation or gender identity of another who would prefer to keep this information secret."

-Wherever a person might be in this process should be respected. It can be very damaging to people who are part of the LGBTQ+ community to ignore this and make their sexuality public. It should be noted that the coming out process is not automatically the same for everyone. A gay man might have a very different coming out process when compared to a trans man.

Offensive terms

Gay as a description is not appropriate. It means that negative qualities are being attributed to being gay, therefore substituting the word "gay" in place of a negative word used to describe a person or situation.

Tranny

Tranny is an extremely offensive word. It is not a word that should be used to describe a trans person, or as a joke.

Faggot

It should come without saying that this word is often use as a serious offense against gay and other LGBTQ people, it is **not** a word that should be used in any setting.

There are many terms that can be offensive, it is always best to have the person that is from the LGBTQ+ community decide which terms they want to use.

LGBTQ+ terminology video

https://www.youtube.com/watch?v=tRvFj3ugdWU

Common Stereotypes

When you think about the LGBTQ+ community what stereotypes come to mind?

Are there any positive stereotypes? Please list them

How about negative? Please list the ones you know

The LGBTQ+ community is promiscuous

This has a been a stereotype that has been around for a long time. There is no real evidence showing that this community is any more "sexual" than the heterosexual community.

All gay men are feminine

This stereotype is tied to the idea that somehow sexual attraction will give homosexual men characteristics that are more "female." Gay men can look and be like any other man, their sexuality does not define whether or not they are feminine.

Gay=AIDS

This is a heterosexist stereotype that ignores the transmission of this disease. The transition can happen to anyone, not just gay men. It is also not taken into consideration that gay men are over represented when it comes to AIDS. Being homosexual comes with pressures that might lead one to take part in behaviors that are not associated with sexuality that increase the risk of contracting AIDS.

There have been different studies that have discarded this stereotype, and have confirmed that there is no evidence suggesting that children with same sex parents have any sort of developmental problems when compared with those of heterosexual partnerships. According to CNN a recent study in the Journal of Developmental and Behavioral Pediatrics found that there is no evidence in emotional and physical health when comparing children of same sex parents to those of heterosexual parents.

Being LGBTQ+ is a matter of choice

This stereotype is often at the center of almost anything LGBTQ+ related. Numerous sources have proven that being a person who is part of the LGBTQ+ community did not suddenly decide they were going to be gay, or transgender, but that it is something that they were born with. According to research by the American Psychological Association cited by CNN, both heterosexual and homosexual behaviors are normal expressions of human sexuality. The key word in this is *normal.*

LGBTQ+ Stereotypes video

https://www.youtube.com/watch?v=wCjZvpya470

Conclusion

LGBTQ+ Americans are a group that is still fighting for basic human rights in most parts of our country. They are often discriminated against and are commonly victims of hate crimes. This population has many stereotypes and misinformation surrounding it. Change for the better can come not only from being aware, but from also passing that awareness onto others that are misinformed.

References

1) Lesbian, Gay, Bisexual, Transgender, Queer, Intersex, Asexual Resource Center. (n.d.). Retrieved July 05, 2017, from https://lgbtqia.ucdavis.edu/educated/glossary.html

2) Modern science says homosexuality is not a choice. (2014, December 31). Retrieved July 08, 2017, from http://www.washingtontimes.com/news/2014/dec/31/modern-science-says-homosexuality-not-choice/

3) Kounang, N. (2016, April 15). No effect for kids of same-sex parents. Retrieved July 01, 2017, from http://www.cnn.com/2016/04/15/health/health-of-children-with-same-sex-parents/index.html

CHAPTER 17
CONCLUSION

Cultural competence doesn't just naturally occur in most people; rather, cultural competence must be intentionally addressed through education. Furthermore, cultural competence development is a lifelong process – one doesn't become magically culturally competent after completing one course or going on an education abroad experience in another country. Thus, it ultimately becomes important to think about how one can develop an intercultural lifestyle which regularly incorporates ways in which to learn culturally on a daily basis. Such an intercultural lifestyle would ideally mean that one has developed relationships with people from a variety of different backgrounds, and continues to seek out new information, regardless of how experienced or knowledgeable one becomes about other cultures.

As humanity faces many daunting issues that impact on our very survival, the development of culturally competence becomes even more urgent.

DISCUSSION QUESTIONS

Reflect on how your personal experiences with culture and difference shaped your conception of yourself as a professional.

1. How might a person's cultural and racial experiences influence their career path?

2. Share with a colleague or two some of the ways in which your experiences with culture and difference influenced your career choice.

3. How have these experiences shaped your views of students who are from racial and cultural groups different from your own?

Tips on How to Become More Culturally Competent

1. Learn about your culture and values, focusing on how they inform your attitudes, behavior, and verbal and nonverbal communication.

2. Don't place "good" and "right" values in your own culture exclusively; acknowledge that the beliefs and practices of other cultures are just as valid.

3. Question your cultural assumptions: Check their reality, rather than immediately acting on them.

4. Accept cultures different from your own and understand that those differences can be learned.

5. Learn to contrast other cultures and values with your own.

6. Learn to assess whether differences of opinion are based on style (communication, learning, or conflict) or substance (issue).

7. Examine the circle in which you live and play (this reflects your choice of peers). Expand your circle to experience other cultures, values, and beliefs.

8. Continue to read and learn about other cultures. Do your homework: Know something about another culture group prior to approaching them.

9. Follow appropriate protocol: Know and demonstrate respectful behavior based on the values of the group.

10. Use collaborative networks—church (spiritual), community, or other natural support groups of that culture.

11. Practice respect.

12. Understand that any change or new learning experience can be challenging, unsettling, and tiresome; give yourself a break and allow for mistakes.

13. Remember the reciprocal nature of relationships—give something back.

14. See multiculturalism as an exciting, fulfilling, and resourceful way to live.

15. Have fun and keep your sense of humor!